elegant Ribbonwork

Helen Gibb

©2006 Helen Gibb

Published by

krause publications
An Imprint of F+W Publications

700 East State Street • Iola, WI 54990-0001
715-445-2214 • 888-457-2873

Our toll-free number to place an order or obtain a free catalog is (800) 258-0929.

A note about the cover photo:
Ribbon roses, blossoms, rosettes and leaves are made
using a variety of vintage ribbonwork techniques.

The following registered trademark terms and companies appear in this publication:
Ultrasuede©, Aleene's© Tacky Glue©, E-6000© and Velcro©.

Library of Congress Catalog Number: 2006929410

ISBN 13-digit: 978-0-89689-310-8
ISBN 10-digit: 0-89689-310-3

Edited by Susan Sliwicki
Designed by Heidi Bittner-Zastrow
Photographs by Brandon Wade
Illustrations by Karen Wallach and Helen Gibb

Printed in China

Credits

Heartfelt thanks to all of the people involved with this book, in particular:

Brandon Wade, for the beautiful photographs; my editor, Susan Sliwicki, who fixed my errors and graciously allowed a deadline extension; Beth Hill, for her wonderful half dolls; Brooke Exley of Hanah Silk, for supporting my work and for making available to me the beautiful bias-cut silk ribbons; Marge Boyle at Quilters Resource Inc., who keeps us all supplied with French ribbons and notions for ribbonwork; Renaissance Ribbons, which continues to bring us beautiful French ribbons and trims; and Mokuba, which makes many of the scrumptious ribbons used in several of the projects in this book.

Thanks to Valarie Beers, for the use of two bridal photos.
Thanks also go to Mary Frances Dreyer and Candace Fouts at the Fuzzy Antler, for allowing us to photograph a few of the projects in their beautiful shop.

Special thanks to Cynthia Anaya, Elaine Brunjes, Peter and Nola Ford, Sue Ford, Diane Fugit, Anita Gibb, Jenny Hawkins, Jenni Hlawatsch, Joyce Hoffsetz, Irene Johnson, Mary Jo Manes, Liz Morath and Linda Murdoch.

Loving thanks to my husband, Jim, who once again has endured my book writing ups and downs; and to my daughter, Melinda, for being the perfect 1920s model. I love you both.

Dedication

To my daughter, Melinda.
You are such a creative
and talented woman.

Table of Contents

Chapter 5
More Elegant Ribbonwork ... 60

Chapter 6
Techniques Guide 100

A Note from the Author

porate ribbon roses, the most classical and beautiful of all ribbonwork flowers. I should have named the book "The Ultimate Ribbon Rose Project Book!" While some of my "tried and true" ribbon roses are used in new ways in the projects, there are several new rose techniques that have never been published before. These new roses grace the cover of the book, as well as a brooch, a lampshade and an opera jacket. I think you will enjoy making and using these new roses on your projects.

The addition of ribbons, trims and dainty ribbon flowers to embellish many beautiful garments and decorative items is timeless. Ribbonwork from the 1920s has been especially inspiring for me, and it is from these vintage treasures — boxes, dresses, hats and half dolls — that I have adapted and created the embellishments for new projects such as the ones found in this book. Some of these items include wedding gowns, scarves, jackets, hats, anniversary albums, brooches, bracelets, tassels and more.

As you look through the pages of this book, you'll notice that all but one of the projects incor-

Large silk satin rose from a boudoir pillow. Circa 1930.

The projects in the book are arranged in three sections — wedding, special occasion, and delightful miscellany. While some of the projects seem specific — for example, wedding — be open-minded about the use of the flowers. You might find that the roses used in the wedding bouquet might look equally beautiful in another color and used on a pillow or a hat box!

The projects range in skill levels from easy to more challenging, with everything quite achievable once you have an understanding of the techniques. Be sure to take the time to read about the special supplies needed for ribbonwork, the

Three small ribbon roses and leaves are combined together to make a corsage for use on a jacket lapel.

tips in getting started, and in particular, the ribbon techniques. Once you are ready to begin the projects, you'll notice that each project in the book gives you a supply list and steps to complete the project. You'll also notice that the steps give the basic flower methods and then refer you back to Chapter 6 — Techniques Guide for instructions on making the actual flower components.

Consider this book a creative journey into the world of elegant ribbonwork. Enjoy using exquisite ribbons to make the flowers and to create the projects, and before long, you will accumulate a treasure trove of heirlooms to hand down to the next generation.

Helen

P.S. I was thrilled when my daughter presented me with a very special ribbonwork gift. It's not a ribbon flower—it's a poem. Immerse yourself in poetic ribbonwork on page 8.

Vintage lounging robe with pockets encrusted with ribbon flowers. Circa 1920.

Ribbonwork

I run my finger over
the sheen of silken threads
woven tightly together
in soft, ombre hues.

I draw out a few inches revealing
light's luminescence on ribbon.
As sharp scissors angle a cut,
a timeless tradition emerges.

I begin my work with folds and gathers;
thread and thimble.
Decades past unfold before me;
echoes of brooches and purses.

Heaps of findings and beads;
piles of crinoline and lace.
I fashion flowers and leaves through
knots, twists and ruching.

I pin my creation to a jacket's lapel
and the 1920s woman inside me smiles.
Classic ribbon and simple stitches
breathe new life into vintage artistry.

Melinda E. Hand

Chapter 1
A Window to the Past

1920s boudoir dolls, powder boxes, chatelaines and half dolls.

amples of ribbonwork from the 1920s are not easily found, but the pieces that decorate the pages of this book will give you an idea of what was done. Sadly, many of the pieces we see today are no longer in pristine condition, but it is still wonderful to see the ribbon creations stitched by women of a bygone age.

Much of the ribbonwork that was done was used to decorate candy boxes, pillows, dresses, candlestick lamps, powder boxes, evening bags, lingerie, blouses, handkerchief cases, half doll pincushions and tea cozies.

Popular books at the time were a series of domestic arts books published by the Woman's Institute of Domestic Arts and Sciences that included sections on ribbonwork. Another series of booklets, titled "Ribbon Art," contained page after page of ribbon projects that included ribbon flowers for garments, headbands, girdles, hats, purses, half dolls and more. Rarely are these publications found intact, if at all.

Enjoy this small gallery of vintage ribbonwork, mostly from the 1920s, and be inspired by the artistry of a past era.

A large basket of velvet ribbon flowers on fabric is newly framed with vintage metallic braid.

Clip-on lampshades, silk-covered wire box and ribbonwork are sewn to a newly made pincushion using vintage fabrics and trims.

Six roses adorn a ribbon basket. The roses are made of ribbon that has been twisted and spiraled into a rose shape.

Multiple flowers made from a variety of ribbon in a thread woven basket are stitched to fabric-covered crinoline.

Porcelain half doll made into a milk jug cover. Australian, circa 1920.

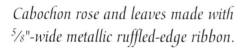

Cabochon rose and leaves made with ⅝"-wide metallic ruffled-edge ribbon.

Rose made with silk satin fabric covered in metallic mesh.

Tiny flat rose with petals made with metallic ribbon and embellished with rhinestones.

Velvet boudoir pillow decorated with large pink satin roses.

Fancy drawstring purse with metallic lace, tassels and ribbon flower trim. A mirror is sewn to the underside of the purse.

English candy box with dimensional roses.
Each rose is made with individual
stemmed petals.
Note that the rose ribbon has whipstitched
thread along its edge.

Rolled-edge roses and blossoms made with a variety of ribbons are combined in a spray on a crinoline.

French candy box with metallic lace, braid,
tassels and ribbon flower trim.

Detail of a pocket from a 1920s lounging robe,
featuring a rose with rolled petals and
a mix of rosettes and blossoms.

Powder puff holder with mirror on the underside
of the "purse." Small silk folded roses, blossoms
and leaves decorate the front of the holder.

Brightly colored silk ribbon fuchsias trim a pleated fabric ruff.

Chapter 2
Before You Begin

Ribbonwork tools and supplies.

Supplies for Ribbonwork

Basic Supplies

For the best results in ribbonwork, have the following supplies on hand:

- **Milliner's needles, size no. 10,** are long and very thin needles with very small eyes so they slide through ribbon without leaving holes. Most seed beads will fit over these needles, so you won't have to switch to a beading needle when adding beads to a ribbon flower center.

- **Twisted beading thread** is thin and strong, and it gathers the ribbon tightly without breaking. White thread is used for most ribbon colors; if ribbons are very dark, then black thread may be used. Most of the stitches in ribbonwork are hidden in the folds of the ribbon, not seen.

- **Ultra-thin long pins** can hold a lot of ribbon and act as an extra set of "fingers" when keeping ribbonwork pieces in place before they are stitched to a project.

- **Crinoline** is a very stiff, open-weave fabric, similar to buckram, but lighter weight. Sometimes, crinoline is used as a base to make one flower, such as a cabochon rose, a flat rose or a coil rose. Other times, crinoline is the base onto which individual flowers and leaves are stitched to form a floral composition. After the composition is complete, the remaining crinoline is carefully cut away around the flowers and leaves. The composition is then tacked to the garment or surface needing embellishment.

- **Scissors** in two styles — a sharp pair for cutting ribbon and a pair of embroidery scissors for cutting threads — are needed.

- **A ruler or tape measure** is needed to measure lengths of ribbon. It is a good idea to have the ruler or tape measure markings in both inches and millimeters/centimeters.

- **Seed beads** in a selection of flower colors, crystal, gold and pearl are very useful. Beads add sparkle and dimension to the ribbon composition. The beads can be used as flower centers or as dangles in a brooch composition. Or, a larger bead can be added to a large flower as a dewdrop.

- **Stamens** are used in the centers of flowers. They are sold double-headed in a variety of colors.

- **A pincushion** is handy to hold pins and threaded needles so they are ready for use at all times.

- **Thread-covered wire** is used for some flower stems. Keep sizes 32-, 22-, 20- and 18-gauge on hand. The highest-number wire is the thinnest wire; it is best suited for small flower stems, such as blossoms and rosettes. Big flowers, such as roses, need 20- or 18-gauge wire stems.

- **A pair of needle-nose wire cutters** is best for cutting wire. The pointed end is useful for making small loops in the wire.

- **Floral tape or bias-cut silk ribbon** is used to cover the stems. The floral tape works if the flowers are used in a vase, and the bias-cut silk ribbon is the best choice if the flowers are used on clothing, hats, purses or fabric backgrounds.

- **Craft glue** is not used to make ribbon flowers, but it is used to cover the stem of a flower with bias-cut silk ribbon. Aleene's Tacky Glue dries clear and works well.

- **Clear, multipurpose adhesive** is used on the Ribbon Bracelet project. E-6000 works well.

Ribbons

The real beauty in a ribbonwork composition of flowers is the use of a variety of ribbons and techniques. Ribbons come in many styles and widths, with the very best ribbons made in France and Japan. While it is tempting to learn ribbonwork with cheaper craft ribbons, it is not advised, as a soft, supple touch to the ribbon is essential for successful ribbonwork. Sources for ribbons are in the Resources section at the back of this book.

Eleven different styles of ribbon and trim with lace leaves are used to make this charming ribbon flower composition.

Ribbon Types Used in This Book

- **Wire-edge ribbon** is a basic ribbon available in widths of ⅝", 1" and 1½", and it is suited for most of the techniques found in this book. Wired ribbon has a very thin copper wire encased in the edges of the ribbon. The ribbons can be used with or without the wire according to the technique. Sometimes, a certain stitching technique requires the removal of the wire if it's next to the stitching or gathering line. To remove the wire from the ribbon, simply expose the copper wire at the raw edge and gently pull the wire out.

- **Bias-cut silk ribbon** — ribbon cut on the bias — has a raw edge (suitable for fraying) and is available in five widths ranging from ⁷⁄₁₆" to 2½". It is suitable for most techniques.

- **Jacquard ribbons**, which are woven with a design, are not used for flower making, but they are used for embellishing and as backgrounds for ribbon flowers.

- **Double-face silk satins, pleated ribbons, velvet ribbons, picot and ruffle-edge ribbons** come in widths ranging from ¼" to 1½".

- **Embroidery-type silk ribbons** in widths of 7 mm (¼"), 13 mm (½") and 36 mm (1½") are also good to use.

As a general rule, ribbons that are 1" and 1½" wide are suitable for the larger flowers and leaves, while the smaller flowers and leaves use ribbon widths ranging from ¼" to ¾".

Select a variety of colors in as many widths and styles as are available; buy 1 yd. of the narrower-width ribbons and at least 2 yd. of the wider-width ribbons. Select a range of pinks, plums, peaches, yellows, blues, purples, creams and greens. Buy as many different green ribbons as you can find! Also, purchase several styles of flower bud trims, as these often can be substitutes for flowers in very small compositions.

Ribbon Miscellany

- **Ironing:** Ribbons can be ironed. Use a pressing cloth over the ribbon and the lightest setting on the iron.
- **Storage:** Store your ribbons in small boxes lined with acid-free paper. Or, use medium-size plastic bins with lids. Spool the ribbon around your fingers, and set the ribbons in the container in neat rows according to color.
- **Steaming:** If ribbon flowers become squashed, a gentle steaming will bring them back to life.
- **Cleaning:** Most ribbonwork won't need cleaning. If a garment with ribbonwork needs cleaning, remove the embellishment.
- **Removing wire:** To remove the wire from the ribbon, simply expose the copper wire at the raw edge, and gently pull the wire out.
- **Fixing frayed edges:** When ribbon is cut, it sometimes produces frayed, "hairy" edges after a little use. Simply cut off the offending threads and keep sewing.

A Few Beginning Tips

- Keep several needles threaded and ready to use in your pincushion.
- Use a single thread for stitching. A length of 20" or so is best, as the thread is short enough to work quickly and is least likely to get a knot.
- Try to work out a knot by pulling tightly on the thread. If it won't "snap" out, then cut the thread and start again.
- Start any stitching at least ⅛" in from a raw edge. If the edge is finished, you can stitch right alongside it.
- If the ribbon has a wired edge and you are going to sew or gather along that edge, then remove the wire. The gathering will be much nicer and fuller.
- Left-handers should feel free to stitch and fold ribbons from whichever direction is most comfortable.
- A final thought: Ribbonwork is not something you rush through. Give yourself time to become used to working with lightweight ribbons, skinny needles and new techniques. The "all thumbs" feeling will soon disappear.

A small bouquet of folded roses and rosettes sit upon a small bow with streamers. Bead dangles add movement and elegance to the overall composition.

Stitches

Most ribbonwork can be accomplished by using backstitches, running stitches (also called gathering stitches) and stab stitches.

Backstitch

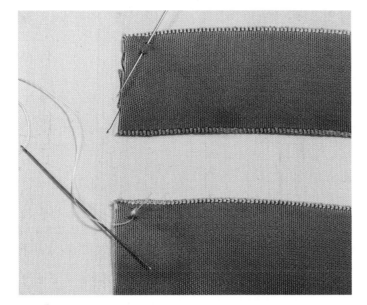

Using a backstitch replaces the need for a knot to anchor the thread in the ribbon. Knots pull out!

1. Start with the needle at the top of the woven ribbon edge and a generous ⅛" or ¼" in from the raw edge. Scoop up a little bit of ribbon onto the needle, pull the thread through and leave a ½" thread tail.

2. Repeat the stitch in the same spot three more times. Gently tug on the thread to be sure it will hold.

3. Proceed with the running stitch or whatever task is required.

4. After the ribbon is gathered, secure the gathering with the same backstitch procedure. Closely trim the excess thread tails.

Running or Gathering Stitch

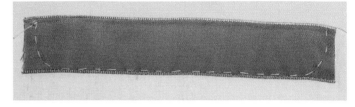

A running stitch or gathering stitch is used to gather the ribbon.

1. Anchor the thread in the ribbon with backstitches rather than a knot.

2. Take at least three or four stitches at one time before pulling the thread through the ribbon, and stitch very close to the bottom edge of the ribbon if it has a woven edge. Stitch ⅛" from the bottom edge of the ribbon if it is a raw edge or a bias-cut ribbon.

3. To end your gathering or stitching, use a backstitch.

Stab Stitch

The stab stitch is used when sewing (tacking) the flowers and leaves to the crinoline or background fabric. The back view of the ribbon flower composition (above) shows the stab/tacking stitches taken to secure the flowers and leaves to the crinoline. The crinoline is cut away after all the flowers and leaves are attached.

1. After anchoring the thread with backstitches in the back of a flower, take the needle straight down ("stab") through the crinoline or background fabric. Bring the needle back up through both the background fabric and the flower so the stitch is hidden.

2. Repeat this stitch twice more so the flower is secure at its center. Without cutting the thread, simply carry it across the crinoline to where the next flower or leaf will be sewn. Don't tack down the edges of the flowers or leaves until all of the elements have been tacked on.

Stitch Length

Stitch length varies according to the width of the ribbon. The top ribbon in the photo is a ¼"-wide ruffle-edge ribbon. The bottom ribbon is 1"-wide wire-edge ribbon with the wire removed from the gathering edge. Note that the stitching for both ribbons starts ⅛" in from the raw edge and then goes right along the woven edge. The stitch pattern illustrated is the single U-gather.

The wider the ribbon, the larger the stitch length. The narrower the ribbon, the smaller the stitch length. If the stitches are too big, the ribbon will look pleated rather than gathered. There's a happy medium that you will only discover after some practice.

Beginnings and Endings for Cut Edges of Ribbon

All ribbons have two cut edges — raw edges — that need to be dealt with in the flower- and leaf- making process. These raw ends have to be absorbed into the ribbon flower technique somehow or other. Most of the techniques for making flowers and leaves incorporate one or both of the following methods:

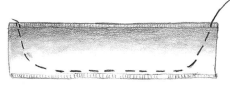

Method 1: Stitch the cut edge so it becomes part of the bottom stitch line after the ribbon is gathered.

Method 2: Fold the cut end down into the sewing line, then proceed with the needed technique. Finish the other cut end of the ribbon as indicated by the technique.

Chapter 3

Ribbonwork for Weddings

Esther Maude Cochrane, Australia, Oct. 21, 1902. Great-grandmother of Helen Gibb.

Myee Ford (nee Moore) left, matron of honor at her sister's wedding. Australia, 1935. Grandmother of Helen Gibb.

Nola and Peter Ford, Australia, Sept. 2, 1950. Parents of Helen Gibb.

A miniature silk shoe filled with waxed Victorian orange blossoms and beaded stems. Circa 1900.

Melinda Hand (nee Gibb), Sept. 18, 2004. Daughter of Helen Gibb.

Wedding Bouquet

When one rose is made using different-colored ribbons and two or three petal techniques, the result is very realistic. This bridal bouquet has eight roses held in a sterling silver tussy mussy. Antique bridal veil, circa 1890.

The blended tea rose, named for the variety of ribbon combinations and techniques used in its construction, will yield spectacular results, as is evident in this bridal bouquet. Of these eight roses, five are made with a mix of pink and cream bias-cut silk satin ribbons, and three are made with a mix of pink wire-edge ribbons. The techniques used for all of the roses are the four-petal U-gather, the single U-gather, and the rolled corner petal techniques. The wire stems (not seen) are wrapped in bias-cut silk ribbon and then inserted into olive green bias-cut silk cording.

While these eight roses are carried in a sterling silver tussy mussy (Victorian flower holder), an alternative would be to tie a beautiful silk ribbon around the stems.

For simplicity, the instructions describe making one rose using two colors of bias-cut silk ribbon. If you are using wire-edge ribbon, use an ombre pink and a solid pink, and follow the same instructions as for the bias-cut silk rose.

You Will Need (For One Rose)

22½" creamy pink bias-cut silk ribbon, 1" wide

35½" creamy pink bias-cut silk satin ribbon, 1½" wide

37½" pale pink bias-cut silk satin ribbon, 1½" wide

12" olive green bias-cut silk ribbon, ⅝" wide

9" olive green silk cording, ¼" wide

20 stamens: 13 yellow, 3 yellow/red tips and
  4 yellow/white tips

4" length thread-covered wire, 32 gauge

9" length thread-covered wire, 18 gauge

Steps

Diagrams are found in Chapter 6 — Techniques Guide.

Flowers

1. Use 20 mixed stamens, and make a stemmed stamen center for the rose. Refer to diagrams 1, 3 and 4. Attach the stamens to 4" of 32-gauge thread-covered wire. After the 4" stamen stem is made, glue it to a 9" piece of 18-gauge thread-covered wire. Set the stem aside until all of the rows of petals are made.

2. Using the ribbon widths and lengths below, make the petals. Group the petals according to their row number.

Row 1

One four-petal U-gather using 8½" of 1"-wide creamy pink bias-cut silk ribbon. Refer to diagrams 40 and 41.

Row 2

Four single U-gather petals using 3½" of 1"-wide creamy pink bias-cut silk ribbon per petal. Refer to diagrams 21 and 24.

Row 3

Five rolled corner petals — four using 3½" of 1½"-wide creamy pink bias-cut silk satin ribbon per petal, and one using 3½" of 1½"-wide pale pink bias-cut silk satin ribbon. Refer to diagrams 58 through 65 for this row of petals, and also for Rows 4 and 5.

Row 4

Six rolled corner petals — two using 4" of 1½"-wide creamy pink bias-cut silk satin ribbon and four using 4" of 1½"-wide pale pink bias-cut silk satin ribbon.

Row 5

Seven rolled corner petals—three using 4½" of

1½"-wide creamy pink bias-cut silk satin ribbon and four using 4½" of 1½"-wide pale pink bias-cut silk satin ribbon.

3. Stitch the first row of continuous petals tightly to the stamen center. Stitch the second row of single U-gather petals to the previous row of petals. Sew through the base of all of the petals to secure them tightly to the stem.

4. Working clockwise, sew the rolled corner petals to the rose base in row order. Mix the order of the petal color within a row as desired. The petals will overlap each other. The petals will be positioned slightly higher than the top of the rose center. Do not let the petals slip down the stem as you sew them onto the previous row. From time to time, stitch through all of the layers of ribbon at the base, and pull the thread tightly.

Putting It All Together

1. When the rose is complete, smear a little glue on the underside of the rose and stem. Wrap the raw edges of the rose and down the stem with the olive green bias-cut silk ribbon (as you would use floral tape).

2. To give the rose stem a thicker look, slip a 9" length of olive green bias-cut silk cording over the stem, and secure it with a little craft glue at the top of the stem.

Bridal Roses
for a Wedding Gown

*Using a mix of 1½"- and 2½"-wide bias-cut silk ribbons
and two techniques, these silk roses make a stunning arrangement
for the back of a wedding gown.*

eddings and roses are a timeless combination, and it's pure elegance when these silk roses adorn the back of a wedding gown. There are four bridal roses in this arrangement – one large, two medium and one small. Each rose is made using bias-cut satin silk ribbons on a wire stem. The stemmed roses and leaves are joined together to make one "bouquet," which is then pinned to the back of the gown for easy removal.

You Will Need

72" ivory bias-cut silk ribbon, ⅝" wide
48" ivory bias-cut silk ribbon, 1½" wide
123" ivory bias-cut silk satin ribbon, 2½" wide
12" ivory bias-cut silk satin ribbon, 1½" wide
16" thread-covered wire, 20 gauge
15" thread-covered wire, 32 gauge
White floral tape
2 small safety pins

Steps

Diagrams are found in Chapter 6 — Techniques Guide.

Flowers and Leaves

1. Make the bridal roses in two parts: a folded rose center and rolled corner petals. Make four folded rose centers using 12" of 1½"-wide ivory bias-cut silk ribbon per rose and the folded rose technique; see diagrams 52 through 57. Glue a 4" length of 20-gauge wire into the first fold of the ribbon when making the center.

2. Make the rolled corner petals; see diagrams 58 through 65. Make 12 small petals using 4" of 2½"-wide ivory bias-cut silk satin ribbon per petal. Make nine medium petals using 5" of 2½"-wide ivory bias-cut silk satin ribbon per petal. Make five large petals using 6" of 2½"-wide ivory bias-cut silk satin ribbon per petal. Separate the petals according to their size.

3. Combine the rose center and petals to complete the rose.

Small Rose

Sew three small petals around the folded rose center. The petals will be positioned slightly higher than the top of the rose center. Cover the base of the petals and down the stem wire with bias silk ribbon.

Medium Rose

Make the same as the small rose, and add a second row of three medium petals. Cover the base of the petals and down the stem wire with bias silk ribbon.

Large Rose

Make the same as the medium rose and add a third row of five large petals. Cover the base of the petals and down the stem wire with bias silk ribbon.

4. Make three crossover leaves using 4" of 1½"-wide ivory bias-cut silk satin ribbon and the crossover leaf technique; see diagrams 83 through 85. Insert a 5" piece of 32-gauge wire into the gathering edge before tightly securing.

5. Cover the base of the leaves and down the stem wire with the ⅝"-wide ivory bias-cut silk ribbon.

Putting It All Together

1. Combine the four stemmed roses and three stemmed leaves into one spray, and bind them together with white floral tape.

2. For a lovely finish, cover the tape with the ⅝"-wide ivory bias-cut silk ribbon. Sew two safety pins to the back of the arrangement so it attaches easily to the gown.

Corsage
for a Bridal Gown

*A simple corsage of ribbon roses can be used on
the front of a bridal gown, worn by the mother of the bride
or given as special thank-yous to the bridesmaids.*

Add a very simple rose corsage to the front or waist of any wedding gown. This corsage, made up of a medium and a small rose with three leaves, is made exactly like the Bridal Roses for a Wedding Gown, page 26. These lovely roses might also be used on a ring bearer pillow or atop a cake. The roses are made with bias-cut silk ribbons for a softer, more luxurious look. Wire-edge ribbons could also be used.

You Will Need

36" ivory bias-cut silk ribbon, ⅝" wide
24" ivory bias-cut silk ribbon, 1½" wide
39" ivory bias-cut silk satin ribbon, 2½" wide
12" ivory bias-cut silk satin ribbon, 1½" wide
8" thread-covered wire, 20 gauge
12" thread-covered wire, 32 gauge
White floral tape
1 medium safety pin

Steps

Diagrams are found in Chapter 6 — Techniques Guide.

Flowers and Leaves

1. Make the bridal roses in two parts — a folded rose center and rolled corner petals. Make two rose centers using 12" of 1½"-wide ivory bias-cut silk ribbon per rose and the folded rose technique; refer to diagrams 52 through 57. Insert and glue a 4" length of 20-gauge wire into the first fold of the ribbon when making the center.

2. Make the rolled corner petals; see diagrams 58 through 65. Make six small rolled corner petals using 4" of 2½"-wide ivory bias-cut silk satin ribbon per petal. Make three medium rolled corner petals using 5" of 2½"-wide ivory bias-cut silk satin ribbon per petal. Separate the petals according to their size.

3. Combine the rose center and petals to complete the rose.

Small Rose

Sew three small petals around the folded rose center. The petals will be positioned slightly higher than the top of the rose center. Cover the base of the petals and down the stem wire with bias silk ribbon.

Medium Rose

Make the same as the small rose, and add a second row of three medium petals. Cover the base of the petals and down the stem wire with bias-cut silk ribbon.

4. Make three crossover leaves using 4" of 1½"-wide ivory bias-cut silk satin ribbon and the crossover leaf technique; refer to diagrams 83 through 85. Insert a 4" piece of 32-gauge wire into the gathering edge before tightly securing.

5. Cover the base of the leaves and down the stem wire with the ⅝"-wide ivory bias-cut silk ribbon.

Putting It All Together

1. Combine the two roses and the three leaves into a small spray, and secure them with floral tape. For a lovely finish, cover the stems with more of the ⅝"-wide ivory bias silk ribbon.

2. Sew the safety pin to the back of the corsage.

Roses
in Silver Vase Pin

Small roses in a vase pin are wonderful reminders of a special occasion, whether it's a wedding or an anniversary. For a wedding, consider this type of arrangement as a keepsake for the mother of the bride and mother of the groom.

Three small bridal roses with three prairie point leaves tucked in a sterling silver vase pin are perfect for someone very special. These small arrangements may be used without the vase pin — simply tie a lovely sheer ribbon around the stems, and use a corsage pin to attach it to a jacket, hat, dress or purse.

The three pink roses are made the same way as the Bridal Roses for a Wedding Gown, page 26, only on a much smaller scale. Each rose is made in two parts. A folded rose center is surrounded by three rolled corner petals.

You Will Need

36" creamy pink bias-cut silk ribbon, 1" wide
17½" creamy pink bias-cut silk satin ribbon, 1½" wide
14" pale pink bias-cut silk satin ribbon, 1½" wide
12" pale green wire-edge ribbon, 1½" wide
36" olive green bias-cut silk ribbon, 7/16" wide
21" thread-covered wire, 32 gauge
Vase pin

Steps

Diagrams are found in Chapter 6 — Techniques Guide.
Flowers and Leaves
1. Make three folded roses using 12" of 1"-wide creamy pink bias-cut silk ribbon and the folded rose technique; refer to diagrams 52 through 57. Insert and glue a 3" length of 32-gauge thread-covered wire into the first fold of the ribbon when making the center.

2. Make nine small rolled corner petals — four using 3½" of 1½"-wide pale pink bias-cut silk satin ribbon and five using 3½" of 1½"-wide creamy pink bias-cut silk satin ribbon per petal. Refer to the rolled corner petal technique; see diagrams 58 through 65.

3. Mixing the colors of the petals for each rose, sew three small petals around each folded rose center. The petals will be positioned slightly higher than the top of the rose center.

4. Cover the base of the petals and down the stem wire with green bias silk ribbon.

5. Make three prairie point leaves using 4" of 1½"-wide pale green wire-edge ribbon; refer to diagrams 79 through 82. Insert a 4" piece of 32-gauge wire into the gathering edge before tightly securing.

6. Cover the base of the leaves and down the stem wire with the 7/16"-wide olive green bias-cut silk ribbon.

Putting It All Together
1. Combine the three roses and the three leaves into a small posy. Trim the stem wires to the desired length. Cover the stems with 7/16"-wide olive green bias-cut silk ribbon.

2. Insert the posy into a vase pin, or tie it with a sheer ribbon.

Wedding Veil Headpiece

*Small folded roses are sewn to a strip of ribbon
and attached to bridal veiling, resulting in a simple headpiece.*

Headpieces for bridal veils can be quite simple, like this lovely miniature spray of roses. Make a veil using your own method and attach it to a comb, or purchase a ready-made veil. Decorate the top of the veil or comb with six folded roses and six small curve leaves sewn to a 6" length of ribbon.

You Will Need

72" ivory bias-cut silk ribbon, 1" wide
15" cream double-face silk satin ribbon, ⅜" wide
6" cream double ruffle-edge ribbon, ¾" wide
5" length of hook-and-loop tape
Bridal veil with comb

Steps

Diagrams are found in Chapter 6 — Techniques Guide.

Flowers and Leaves

1. Make six folded roses using 12" of 1"-wide ivory bias-cut silk ribbon per flower and the folded rose technique; see diagrams 52 through 57.

2. Closely trim the raw ends of the finished roses.

3. Make six curve leaves using 2½" of ⅜"-wide cream double-face silk satin ribbon and the curve leaf technique; see diagrams 87 through 90.

4. Fold under ½" at each end of the 6" piece of ¾"-wide double ruffle-edge ribbon, and secure it with very small running stitches.

Putting It All Together

1. Sew the six roses to the ruffle-edge ribbon.

2. Sew three curve leaves to each end of the ruffle-edge ribbon, and tucked them under the roses.

3. Sew a strip of hook-and-loop tape to the underside of the double ruffle-edge ribbon, and attach it to the comb on the veil.

Wedding Guestbook
with Lily of the Valley

*Albums and guestbooks make thoughtful gifts for special occasions.
This guestbook is designed for a wedding and is decorated with very wide
jacquard ribbon, lily of the valley ribbon flowers and a milliner's bow.
Lace veil circa 1890.*

The inspiration for the guestbook came from the beautiful lily of the valley jacquard ribbon. Using this ribbon, cream dupioni silk, a delicate lace edging, a silk satin bow and a small spray of faux lily of the valley ribbon flowers, this album can be created with very little time or effort. While these instructions are for a wedding guestbook, they could be adapted for making differently themed albums by simply changing the ribbons and trims.

You Will Need

1 album or guestbook, 8½" x 6½"

18" x 6½" piece batting, ¼" thin

20" x 8½" piece cream dupioni silk fabric

8" lily of the valley jacquard ribbon, 3" wide

8" off-white lace edging, 2" wide

22" pale green double-face silk satin ribbon, 1" wide

10" off-white ruffle-edge ribbon, ½" wide

1½" square piece of crinoline

15" pale green gimp trim

2 sheets fancy paper, 8" x 6"

Craft glue

Toothpick

Steps

Diagrams are found in Chapter 6 — Techniques Guide.

Book Cover

1. Lightly glue the thin batting over the album's front and back covers. Trim the excess batting so it is flush to the edges of the cover.

2. Cover the book with fabric; use your favorite method.

3. Using a toothpick, dot glue along the straight edge of the lace, and place it on the front cover. The raw ends will fold back to the inside of the book cover. These will be covered with paper later.

4. Smear a small amount of glue along both straight edges of the jacquard ribbon, and place it on top of and to the left of the lace.

Flowers and Bow

1. Make five lily of the valley flowers using 2" of ½"-wide ruffle-edge ribbon and 3" of gimp per flower stem, referring to the tube technique for bell flowers. Refer to diagrams 17 through 20. Stagger the gimp stems, and stitch them together at the top. Trim the excess gimp.

2. Make a four-loop bow. This bow is made in three parts and sewn to crinoline. Make two sets of two loops using 10" of 1"-wide pale green double-face silk satin ribbon per set. Stagger the loops, and eliminate any tails. Refer to diagram 13.

3. Slightly gather the ends, and stitch each set to a 1½" square of crinoline, with raw ends facing each other. Cut away the excess crinoline, and cover the raw edges of the loops with a 2" piece of pale green silk ribbon. Secure it with stitches in the back of the bow.

Putting It All Together

1. Sew the small spray of lily of the valley flowers to the back of the bow. Carefully glue the bow/lilies to the front cover.

2. Finish the inside of the book covers; glue decorative end papers that have been trimmed to size inside each cover.

Chapter 4
Ribbonwork for Fashionable Occasions

Pink Hat with Roses

Scarf and Purse Set

Black Gloves with Double Rosettes

Opera Jacket with Flowers

Pink Hat
with Roses

*Two vintage-style ribbon roses and milliner's velvet leaves
add a touch of glamour to this 1920s-style hat.*

Go out for tea in this charming 1920s-style hat! The large roses are made using just two techniques — U-gather and vintage flat rose. The buds are made using the crossover leaf technique. If hats aren't your cup of tea, then use the roses on a tote or boudoir pillow.

You Will Need

1 hat of your choice

63" taupe pleated crepe georgette ribbon, ⅝" wide

6" pink ruffle-edge ribbon, ¼" wide

52" pink double-face silk satin ribbon, 1¼" wide

12" olive green bias-cut silk ribbon, ⁷⁄₁₆" wide

2 circles of crinoline, 3" diameter

1 circle of crinoline, 1¾" diameter

1 glass button, 1" diameter

8" thread-covered wire, 32 gauge

7 milliner's leaves

Steps

Diagrams are found in Chapter 6 — Techniques Guide.

Flowers and Buds

1. Make a taupe spiral rose. Slightly gather 54" of ⅝"-wide taupe pleated crepe georgette ribbon using the U-gather technique; see diagram 21. Do not secure the gathering yet. On a 3" circle of crinoline, draw a 1¼" circle in the center. Sew the beginning of the gathered ribbon to the drawn circle, spiraling outward until three layers of ruffles are made. Secure the gathering when the spiral is complete. Secure the spiral rows of ribbon to the crinoline. Sew the 1" diameter glass button to the center of the rose. Make a small ruffle using 6" of pink ruffle-edge ribbon and the U-gather technique; refer to diagram 21. Sew this ruffle over the taupe ribbon and under the button. Trim away the excess crinoline.

2. Make a pink petal rose. The rose is made in three parts. Make a vintage flat rose using 18" of 1¼"-wide pink double-face silk satin ribbon and a 1¾" circle of crinoline. Refer to the vintage flat rose technique, diagrams 46 through 51. Trim the excess crinoline, if any. Make six U-gather petals using 4" of 1¼"-wide pink double-face silk satin ribbon per petal and the U-gather technique; refer to diagrams 21 and 24. At the center of the 3" circle of crinoline, draw a 1½"-circle. Evenly arrange and sew the six petals to the drawn circle on the crinoline. Make a ruffle using 9" of taupe pleated crepe georgette ribbon and the U-gather technique; refer to diagram 21. Sew the taupe ruffle over the raw edges of the petals. Sew the flat rose over the taupe ruffle.

3. Make four stemmed pink buds using 2½" of 1¼"-wide pink double-face silk satin ribbon and 2" of 32-gauge thread-covered wire per bud. Refer to diagrams 83 through 85. Insert the wire into the ribbon before you tighten the gathering on the bud. Use 3" of ⁷⁄₁₆"-wide olive green bias-cut silk ribbon to wrap the stems.

Putting It All Together

1. Using the photo as a guide, sew the two large roses to the hat.

2. Sew the sprays of pink/green milliner's leaves under the roses.

3. Sew the rosebuds under the roses in a fanned-out manner.

Button Rose
Brooch

*Brooches are perfect for use not only on jackets,
but as ornaments on hats. This brooch features ribbon roses and blossoms
surrounding a fabulous button-centered rose.*

This brooch is made using five different ribbon flower techniques and two leaf techniques, and it is sewn to crinoline. While it looks stunning on a summer hat, it would be equally lovely on a jacket, a purse or a tote.

You Will Need

21" cinnamon raspberry wire-edge ribbon, 1½" wide

6" pumpkin wire-edge ribbon, ⅝" wide

6½" taupe double-face silk satin ribbon, ⅜" wide

6" plum pleated crepe georgette ribbon, ⅝" wide

7" red/purple ruffle-edge ribbon, ¼" wide

18" olive green ombre wire-edge ribbon, 1" wide

4" green/yellow ruffle-edge ribbon, ¼" wide

5" length of heavy ecru lace, or five leaf lace motifs

20 gold stamens

1 button, 1¾" diameter

7" red rosebud trim

1 blue butterfly button

14 gold seed beads

4" crinoline square

4" felt or ultrasuede square

1½" pin back

Steps

Diagrams are found in Chapter 6 — Techniques Guide.
Flowers and Leaves

1. Make the large rose using six petals, a large button and stamens, with all sewn to a 4" square of crinoline. Prepare two bundles of stamens (10 stamens in each bundle); refer to diagrams 1 and 2. Set these aside until the rose petals are made.

1a. Make five single side-roll petals using 3½" of 1½"-wide cinnamon raspberry wire-edge ribbon for each petal and the single side-roll technique; see diagrams 66 through 70. Make one double side-roll petal (this will be the front petal) using 4" of 1½"-wide cinnamon raspberry wire-edge ribbon and the double side-roll technique; see diagrams 73 through 77. Set aside.

1b. Overlap and sew three single side-roll petals to the center of the 4" square of crinoline in a small arch. Make sure that the rolls are seen at the front.

1c. Fan out and sew the stamens over the three back petals so the heads of the stamens are about halfway up the height of the petal; see diagram 71.

1d. Sew the large button over the stamens so the gold heads just peek over the button. With the rolls showing on the front of the petal, sew the fourth petal to the left side of the button, and sew the fifth petal to the right side of the button. Be sure the raw edges of the petals are tucked under the button. Sew the last petal (double side-roll) between the fourth and fifth petal. Make sure the raw edges of this petal are turned under. Refer to diagram 72. Fold the petal up and over the button, and set the rose aside.

2. Make one upright coil rose using 6" of ½"-wide pumpkin wire-edge ribbon and the upright U-gather technique; refer to diagrams 29 through 32.

3. Make one blossom using 5" of ⅜"-wide taupe double-face silk satin ribbon and the four petal U-gather technique; see diagrams 40 and 41. Sew five seed beads to the center of the flower. Sew this blossom to the center of the plum pleated rosette.

4. Make one pleated rosette using 6" of ⅝"-wide plum pleated crepe georgette ribbon and the U-gather technique; see diagrams 21 through 23. The taupe blossom is sewn to the center of this rosette.

5. Make three rosettes using 2¼" of ¼"-wide red/purple ruffle-edge ribbon and the U-gather technique; see diagrams 21 through 23 and 26. Sew three seed beads to the center of each rosette.

6. Make seven prairie point leaves using 2½" of 1"-wide olive green ombre wire-edge ribbon for each leaf and the prairie point leaf technique; see diagrams 79 through 82.

7. Make two curve leaves using 2" of ¼"-wide green/yellow ruffle-edge ribbon for each leaf and the curve leaf technique; see diagrams 87 through 90.

Putting It All Together

1. Using the photo as a guide, sew the lace (or lace leaves) to the crinoline, under the base of the main rose.

2. Tuck in and sew all of the prairie point leaves in and around the lace.

3. Sew the large purple/taupe blossom, pumpkin coil rose and rosettes on top of the lace.

4. Sew the two small curve leaves near the purple/taupe blossom.

5. Sew a length of red rosebud trim around the bottom of the flowers, and sew a butterfly button to a petal on the main rose.

6. Cut away the excess crinoline, and cover the back with felt. Sew a pin back to the felt.

Ribbon Flower Bracelet

*A small length of fancy ribbon,
embellished with a garden of miniature flowers, beads and buttons,
becomes an elegant bracelet.*

Ribbon bracelets are a great way to use up small amounts of fancy jacquard ribbons, small lengths of narrow ribbons and charming enamel buttons. Seed beads or tiny rhinestone crystals add further embellishment. Other optional ideas are to add a watch face, a large, fancy button or larger ribbon flowers. Small, pre-made ribbon flowers and tiny flower-shaped beads also may be added. The measurements given will fit a wrist size from 6½" to 8", depending on how much ribbon is trimmed off of the main bracelet band.

You Will Need

7" cream jacquard ribbon, 1" wide

7" pale green double-face silk satin ribbon, 1" wide

14" pink/green loop trim

7" pale yellow silk embroidery ribbon, 7 mm wide

4" pink silk embroidery ribbon, 7 mm wide

3" pale apricot/yellow silk embroidery ribbon, 7 mm wide

3" pale pink silk embroidery ribbon, 7 mm wide

3" lavender silk embroidery ribbon, 7 mm wide

9" olive green silk embroidery ribbon, 4 mm wide

2¼" mauve ombre picot-edge ribbon, ¼" wide

2¼" blue ombre picot-edge ribbon, ¼" wide

2¼" apricot ombre picot-edge ribbon, ¼" wide

3 small enamel pansy buttons

2 small enamel blossom buttons

Seed beads in gold, pearl or crystal

2 end bar clamps

5 jump rings

1 lobster claw closure or 1 toggle closure set

Craft glue

Clear, multipurpose adhesive

Steps

Diagrams are found in Chapter 6 — Techniques Guide.

Flowers and Leaves

1. Make two folded roses — one using 4" of 7 mm-wide pink silk embroidery ribbon and one using 4" of 7 mm-wide pale yellow silk embroidery ribbon. Refer to diagrams 52 through 57.

2. Make three ribbon candy roses — one using 3" of 7 mm-wide pale apricot/yellow silk embroidery ribbon; one using 3" of 7 mm-wide pale pink silk embroidery ribbon; and one using 3" of 7 mm-wide lavender silk embroidery ribbon. Refer to the ribbon candy rose technique in diagrams 8 through 10.

3. Make three rosettes — one using 2¼" of ¼"-wide mauve ombre picot-edge ribbon; one using 2¼" of ¼"-wide blue ombre picot-edge ribbon and one using 2¼" of ¼"-wide apricot ombre picot-edge ribbon. Refer to the U-gather technique; see diagrams 21 through 23 and 26. Sew one seed bead or affix a tiny rhinestone to the center of each rosette.

4. Make one rosette using 3" of ¼"-wide pale yellow embroidery silk ribbon and the U-gather technique; refer to diagrams 21 through 23 and 26. Sew one seed bead, or affix a tiny rhinestone to the center of the flower.

5. Make three figure-eight leaves using 3" of 4 mm-wide olive green silk embroidery ribbon per leaf. See diagrams 15 through 16.

Putting It All Together

1. You will only decorate 4" to 5" of the cream jacquard ribbon band. Using the photo as a guide, sew the largest flowers to the middle of the ribbon band. Follow with the smaller flowers and figure-eight loop leaves; be sure the flowers overlap. Add the enamel buttons, then add the seed beads or rhinestones.

2. Using small stitches, sew the pink/green loop trim to both edges of the cream jacquard ribbon.

3. Sew the green silk satin ribbon to the back of the ribbon band so all of the rough stitching is covered.

4. Measure the bracelet to fit your wrist, allowing approximately 1½" for the jewelry closures. Trim off the excess ribbon at each end, if needed. If you find you have cut the ribbon too short, simply add a few more jump rings to the jewelry closure.

5. Slightly gather across each of the raw ends of the ribbon band so the band fits the width of the end clamps. Trim the raw ends of the ribbon if they are straggly, then glue each raw end with craft glue and let them dry.

6. Using clear multipurpose adhesive, carefully glue inside the end clamp closures. Insert the ribbon ends into the metal end clamps. Squeeze the end clamps closed. Let the piece dry for several hours.

7. Attach one jump ring and the lobster claw or toggle closure to one end clamp. Attach the other jump rings to the other end clamp.

Scarf
and Purse Set

*A ready-made scarf and drawstring purse
are easily embellished with Venice lace, flower trim
and handmade ribbon flowers.*

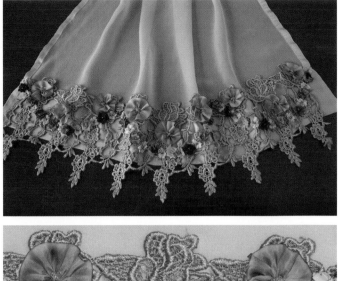

Sometimes it's nice to have something really wonderful to accessorize an outfit. This scarf and drawstring purse in spring green with bright little flowers would look lovely with a simple evening gown or even a fancy tea dress. The bias-cut silk ribbon rosettes and mini-ribbon candy roses on a bed of flower trim are very simple to make. The supply list includes quantities for both ends of the scarf and the front of the purse.

You Will Need

1 purchased silk scarf, 22" wide x 76" long
1 purchased drawstring silk purse 6½" wide x 5½" long
50½" Venice lace, 5½" deep
63" yellow flower trim
153" pink/peach bias-cut silk ribbon, ⅝" wide
36" magenta bias-cut silk ribbon, ⁷⁄₁₆" wide
36" blue/green bias-cut silk ribbon, ⁷⁄₁₆" wide
40" mauve bias-cut silk ribbon, ⁷⁄₁₆" wide
36" lavender bias-cut silk ribbon, ⁷⁄₁₆" wide
36" wine/yellow bias-cut silk ribbon, ⁷⁄₁₆" wide
28" pink/yellow bias-cut silk ribbon, ⁷⁄₁₆" wide
72" pale green double-face silk satin ribbon, ⅜" wide
42" pale green double-face silk satin ribbon, ⅛" wide
1 package pale peach seed beads
5" tassel fringing, 4" deep

Steps

Diagrams are found in Chapter 6 — Techniques Guide.
Scarf
1. Sew 22" of lace to each end of the scarf. Sew 28" of yellow flower trim over the lace; add a peach seed bead in each yellow flower.

2. Make 18 rosettes (nine for each end of the scarf) using 7" of pink/peach ⅝"-wide bias-cut silk ribbon and the U-gather technique; see diagrams 21 through 23 and 27. Sew six pale peach seed beads in a row to the center of the rosette. Sew another six pale peach seed beads in a row so it crosses over the first row. Using the photo as a guide, sew the rosettes to the scarf.

3. Make 46 ribbon candy roses — 23 for each end of the scarf — using 4" of ⁷⁄₁₆"-wide bias-cut silk ribbon and the ribbon candy rose technique; see diagrams 8 through 10. Make eight roses each in magenta, blue/green, mauve, lavender, wine/yellow, and six roses in pink/yellow. Using the photo as a guide, sew the small ribbon candy roses in any color sequence to the flower trim; add a pale peach seed bead in the center of each rose.

Purse

1. Sew 6½" of lace to the purse front. Sew 7" of yellow flower trim over the lace, using a peach seed bead in each yellow flower.

2. Make three rosettes using 7" of ⅝"-wide pink/peach bias-cut silk ribbon and the U-gather technique; see diagrams 21 through 23 and 27. Sew six pale peach seed beads in a row to the center of the rosette. Sew another six pale peach seed beads in a row so this row crosses over the first row. Using the photo as a guide, sew the rosettes to the purse.

3. Make seven ribbon candy roses using 4" of ⁷⁄₁₆"-wide bias-cut silk ribbon and the ribbon candy rose technique; see diagrams 8 through 10. Make two mauve roses, and one rose each of pink/yellow, blue/green, magenta, wine/yellow and lavender ribbons. Using the photo as a guide, sew the roses to the flower trim, using a pale peach seed bead in the center of each rose.

4. Remove the two drawstrings from the purse. Replace each drawstring with 36" of ⅜"-wide pale green double-face silk satin ribbon.

5. Make a three-loop bow using 12" of ⅛"-wide pale green double-face silk satin ribbon and the loop bow technique; refer to diagram 14. Leave a 3" tail on each bow. Make a plain shoelace bow using 9" of ⅛"-wide pale green double-face silk satin ribbon. Sew the two bows together; the five loops will show at the top. Referring to the bow photo, sew a bow on each side of the purse near the drawstrings.

6. Make a small tassel using 5" of fringing; refer to the fringed tassel method described in the Ornamental Tassels project. Sew the tassel to the bottom of the purse.

Black Gloves
with Double Rosettes

*Vintage gloves are perfect to embellish with pleated ribbon
around the cuffs and a ribbon rosette at each wrist.*

Vintage clothing stores are a gold mine for gloves, such as these black beaded gloves. Add some pleated crepe georgette ribbon and a smart ribbon flower at the wrist, and you'll totally transform these gloves. To round out the look, follow the same techniques to add ribbon and a fancy button to a clutch purse.

You Will Need

1 pair black vintage gloves
36" black pleated crepe georgette ribbon, ⅝"-wide
14" black double-ruffle satin ribbon, ¾" wide
2 small fancy buttons or beads

Steps

Diagrams are found in Chapter 6 — Techniques Guide.

1. For each glove, measure around the top of the glove opening, and add 1" to this measurement. Cut the ⅝"-wide black pleated crepe georgette ribbon to this measurement. For the gloves shown, 10" was used.

2. Pin the ribbon around the top of the glove. Using very small running stitches, sew the ribbon to the glove at the top edge.

3. Make one double rosette for each glove. The rosette is made in two parts. For the back rosette, use 7" of ⅝"-wide black pleated crepe georgette ribbon. For the front rosette use 7" of ¾"-wide black double ruffle-edge ribbon. Both rosettes use the U-gather technique; see diagrams 21 through 23. Slightly offset and sew the satin rosette over the pleated crepe georgette rosette so a pansy shape is formed. Sew a fancy button or bead to the center of the flower.

4. Sew a flower to each glove near the wrist.

Cream Gloves
with Roses

Recycling an old pair of gloves lends itself to many embellishing delights.
These kidskin opera gloves were once quite plain.
Now they are positively elegant.

Cream kidskin gloves were often worn for special occasions in the late 19th and early 20th centuries. Adding exquisite jacquard ribbon to the top of the glove, a ruffle of ribbon and a ribbon flower or two will give a totally new look to the gloves. Any glove that you fancy will work for this project.

You Will Need

1 pair cream leather gloves of your choice
20" cream jacquard ribbon, 2½" wide
16" cream double-face silk satin ribbon, ⅜" wide
40" cream ruffle-edge ribbon, ½" wide

Steps

Diagrams are found in Chapter 6 — Techniques Guide.

Ribbon Trim

1. For each glove, measure around the top of the glove opening and add 1" to this measurement. Cut the jacquard ribbon to this measurement. For the project, 10" was used for each glove.

2. Cut the ½"-wide cream ruffle-edge ribbon the same length as the jacquard ribbon. Sew the ruffle-edge ribbon to the bottom edge of the jacquard ribbon.

3. Pin the jacquard/ruffle-edge ribbon around the glove so the top of the ribbon aligns with the top of the glove edge. The ruffle-edge is at the bottom. The ribbon seam is overlapped along the glove seam. Using very small running stitches, sew the ribbon to the glove along the seam, at the top edge and at the bottom edge.

4. Fold the raw edges of the ribbon to the inside, and then butt the pieces together. Sew this seam with very small, neat stitches.

Flowers

1. For each glove, make two cream roses. The roses are made in two parts — a folded rose for the center and a rosette for the outer ruffle. Make the folded rose center using 4" of ⅜"-wide cream double-face silk satin ribbon per flower and the folded rose technique; see diagrams 52 through 57. Make the outer ruffle using 5" of ⅝"-wide cream ruffle-edge ribbon and the U-gather technique; see diagrams 21 through 23. Leave a small hole at the center of the rosette for the folded rose to fit in. Insert the folded rose into the center of the rosette, and secure the two together with a few stitches at the center.

2. Trim the excess ribbon from the underside of the flower.

Putting It All Together

1. Using the photo as a guide, sew two cream roses to each glove.

Opera Jacket
with Flowers

Antique metallic lace is the perfect background for ribbon roses, blossoms and leaves in a variety of shapes and colors.

Words cannot describe the beauty of this flower-encrusted opera jacket! Actually, stunning would be a very good word for it! The flowers and leaves are made with 28 different ribbons using 10 techniques, which creates a glorious riot of color and elegance. The floral composition on the back of the jacket is a V-shape with three rosebuds dangling from the center. An elongated swath of flowers falls down the right lapel, while a smaller composition graces the left lapel. All is overlaid on antique metallic lace, circa 1880.

To replicate this look, make or purchase a black jacket, and gather together some ribbons and other delicious embellishments. This is the perfect project to use up some of those vintage ribbons, laces and trims that you've been hoarding! The instructions describe how to make all of the flowers and leaves, leaving you to decide if you want to have a lace underlay. While this is not a difficult project, it is rather time consuming, and it would be best executed over several months. Do just a little bit at a time so you are not overwhelmed.

You Will Need

97" pink over-dyed ribbon, 1½" wide

45" blue over-dyed ribbon, 1½" wide

42" pumpkin over-dyed ribbon, 1½" wide

30" pumpkin over-dyed ribbon, ½" wide

30" raspberry/cinnamon ombre wire-edge ribbon,
    1" wide

10" yellow/aqua ombre wire-edge ribbon, 1" wide

6" pink ombre wire-edge ribbon, ⅝" wide

4" pink ombre wire-edge ribbon, 1" wide

6" pink double-face silk satin ribbon, ⅝" wide

29" pink double-face silk satin ribbon, 1" wide

18" pale peach double-face silk satin ribbon, 1" wide

54" mauve velvet ribbon, ¾" wide

36" plum velvet ribbon, ¾" wide

18" pink velvet ribbon, ¾" wide

28" red jacquard ribbon, ¾" wide

6" pink ruffle-edge metallic ribbon, ½" wide

18" wine picot-edge ribbon, ½" wide

5" mauve sheer picot-edge ribbon, 1⅛" wide

18" dark gold pleated crepe georgette ribbon, ⅝" wide

12" plum pleated crepe georgette ribbon, ⅝" wide

6" copper pleated crepe georgette ribbon, ⅝" wide

24" lilac velvet-edge ribbon, ⅝" wide

20" green over-dyed ribbon, 1½" wide

50" olive green ombre wire-edge ribbon, 1" wide

10" dark gold ombre wire-edge ribbon, 1" wide

5" brown/green stripe ombre wire-edge ribbon, 1" wide

33¼" dark green shirred ribbon, ½" wide

36" olive green ruffle-edge metallic ribbon, ½" wide

27" olive green bias-cut silk satin cording, ⅛" diameter

Seed beads in gold, copper and mauve

4 crinoline squares, each 4"

2 crinoline squares, each 3"

6 crinoline squares, each 2½"

Steps

Diagrams are found in Chapter 6 — Techniques Guide.
Flowers and Leaves

1. Make four large vintage petal roses. Each one is made on a 4" square of crinoline, in two parts — a folded rose center (refer to the folded rose technique, diagrams 52 through 57) surrounded by 12 or 13 double side-roll petals (refer to the double side-roll petal, diagrams 73 through 78). The front of the petal is the side with the rolls showing.

1a. Make two large pink vintage petal roses using 10" of 1"-wide raspberry/cinnamon wire-edge ribbon per folded rose center, and 12 double side-roll petals using 3" of 1½"-wide pink over-dyed ribbon for each petal. Add a 13th petal using 3½" of 1½"-wide pink over-dyed ribbon to the front of only one rose. This makes the roses look slightly different from each other.

1b. Make one large pumpkin vintage petal rose using 10" of 1"-wide raspberry/cinnamon wire-edge ribbon for the folded rose center and 12 double side-roll petals using 3" of 1½"-wide pumpkin over-dyed ribbon for each petal.

1c. Make one large blue vintage petal rose using 10" of 1"-wide aqua/yellow wire-edge ribbon for the folded rose center and 12 double side-roll petals using 3" of 1½"-wide blue over-dyed ribbon for each petal.

1d. Put the vintage petal rose together. In the center of the 4" square of crinoline, draw a 1¼"-diameter circle. Using the photos and diagram 78 as guides, overlap and sew eight petals (rolled edges facing you) around the drawn circle. Start a second row by sewing two petals just inside the drawn circle. Sew the folded rose on top of these two petals. Overlap and sew two more petals to the front of the folded rose, making sure that the raw edges of the petals are folded under and don't show. A 13th larger petal may be sewn to the front of the rose if called for.

2. Make two small vintage petal roses. Each one is made on a 3" square of crinoline in two parts, exactly the same as the large petal roses above except draw a ¾" circle in the center of the crinoline. Refer to the same folded rose technique and double side-roll petal technique diagrams.

2a. Make one vintage petal rose in mixed pinks and peach. Use 6" of ⅝"-wide pink ombre wire-edge ribbon for the center folded rose, and make 12 petals from different-colored ribbons — two using 2" of 1"-wide pink ombre wire-edge ribbon per petal; six using 2" of 1"-wide pink double-face silk satin ribbon per petal; and four petals using 2" of 1"-wide pale peach double-face silk satin ribbon per petal. Make a 13th petal using 2½" of 1"-wide pink double-face silk satin ribbon for the front of the rose.

2b. Make another small pink/peach vintage petal rose using a slightly different mix of ribbon colors. Use 6" of ⅝"-wide pink double-face silk satin ribbon for the center folded rose. Make 12 petals — seven using 2" of 1"-wide pink double-face silk satin ribbon per petal and

and five using 2" of 1"-wide pale peach double-face silk satin ribbon per petal. Add a 13th petal using 2½" of 1"-wide pink double-face silk satin ribbon for the front of the rose.

3. Make nine large rosebuds using one double side-roll petal per bud. Refer to diagrams 73 through 77 to make the petal shape. To make the bud from the petal, fold one rolled edge, over the other rolled edge and secure it with stitches. You will see the rolls on the front. Make four pink buds, three blue buds and two pumpkin buds. Make a calyx for each bud using 2" of ½"-wide dark green shirred ribbon. For bud stems, insert a 2½" length of bias silk cording into the calyx before securing the top of the calyx. Select three buds, one of each color, and sew their stems together. This group will be used for the dangling buds at the center of the back composition. When attaching the remaining buds to the jacket, twist the cording for added interest; see diagram 5.

4. Make six vintage flat roses using 18" of ¾"-wide velvet ribbon per flower and a 2½" square of crinoline. The finished diameter of each rose is between 1½" and 2". Refer to the vintage flat rose technique; see diagrams 46 through 51. Make three mauve roses, two plum roses and one pink rose. Trim off the excess crinoline very closely to the ribbon. Any tiny bits of crinoline that show can be folded under when you sew the rose to the project.

5. Make eight upright coil roses; refer to the upright U-gather technique, diagrams 29 through 32. Make four roses using 7" of ¾"-wide red jacquard ribbon per flower. Make three roses using 6" of ½"-wide wine picot-edge ribbon per rose. Make one rose using 6" of ½"-wide pink ruffle-edge metallic ribbon.

6. Make five blossoms using 6" of ½"-wide pumpkin over-dyed ribbon per flower, and the four-petal U-gather technique. See diagrams 40 through 41. Sew five gold seed beads to the center of each flower.

7. Make 10 rosettes — three dark gold, two plum and one copper — using 6" of ⅝"-wide pleated crepe georgette ribbon per flower and the U-gather technique; see diagrams 21 through 23. Make four lilac rosettes using 6" of ⅝"-wide lilac velvet-edge ribbon per flower.

Sew nine seed beads — coordinated with the ribbon color — in the center of each rosette.

8. Make one double rosette using 5" of 1⅛"-wide mauve sheer picot-edge ribbon and the two-thirds fold up U-gather technique; see diagrams 33 through 35. Sew six mauve seed beads to the center.

9. Make 15 curve leaves; refer to the curve leaf technique, diagrams 87 through 90. Make six leaves using 3¼" of ½"-wide dark green shirred ribbon per leaf and nine using 4" of ½"-wide olive green ruffle-edge metallic ribbon per leaf.

10. Make 13 boat leaves using 5" of 1"-wide wire-edge ribbon per leaf. Make 10 olive green leaves, two gold/green leaves and one brown/green stripe leaf. Refer to the boat leaf technique diagrams; see diagrams 91 through 95.

11. Make five crossover leaves using 4" of 1½"-wide green over-dyed ribbon per leaf and the crossover leaf technique diagrams; see diagrams 83 through 85.

Putting It All Together

1. If you are using lace as a background for your flowers, sew this to the garment first.

2. Add the flowers and leaves as listed for each section; all of the flowers and leaves are sewn directly to the garment. You may choose to use fewer flowers than shown. Sew only the center of each flower to the fabric so leaves and other elements can be added underneath. Use the detail photos as a guide to sew the flowers to the jacket. When all of the flowers and leaves are sewn on, go back and tack down every edge of every flower and leaf so it doesn't lift up when worn or curved over a body.

Right Front

1. Flowers: One large pink vintage petal rose, one small pink vintage petal rose, three pink buds, one mauve rosette, one gold rosette, one lilac rosette, one pumpkin blossom, one red upright coil rose, one wine upright coil rose.

2. Leaves: Three olive boat leaves, two crossover leaves, one metallic curve leaf. Connect the small rose and large rose with one olive green cording vine.

Left Front

1. Flowers: Plum vintage flat rose, pumpkin bud, pink bud, red upright coil rose, pink metallic upright coil rose, pumpkin blossom, lilac rosette, gold rosette.

2. Leaves: Three crossover leaves, one metallic green curve leaf, one dark green shirred curve leaf.

Right Front

Left Front

Left Back

1. Flowers: One small peachy/pink vintage petal rose, one large pumpkin vintage petal rose, two blue buds, two mauve vintage flat roses, one mauve picot-edge rosette, one pumpkin blossom, one red upright coil rose, one plum rosette, one lilac rosette.

2. Leaves: Three boat leaves (one olive, one stripe, one gold/green), five green metallic curve leaves, one dark green shirred curve leaf.

Center Back

1. Flowers: One large blue vintage petal rose, three dangling buds (blue, pink, pumpkin), one wine upright coil rose.

2. Leaves: Five olive boat leaves, two dark green shirred curve leaves.

Right Back

1. Flowers: One large pink vintage petal rose, one pink bud, three vintage flat roses (pink, plum, mauve), one lilac rosette, one copper rosette, one gold rosette, two pumpkin blossoms, one red upright coil rose, one wine upright coil rose.

2. Leaves: Three boat leaves (two olive, one gold/green), two green metallic curve leaves, two dark green shirred curve leaves.

Left Back

Center Back

Right Back

Chapter 5
More
Elegant Ribbonwork

Wooden Jewelry Box with Roses

Velvet Brooch Pillow

Anniversary Photo Album

Elizabeth Half Doll Pincushion

Covered
Picnic Basket

*Any basket can be transformed from plain to elegant
with the addition of a silk fabric cover and a wreath of ribbon roses.*

A special picnic takes on new meaning when the food is carried in this stylish picnic basket. Choose any basket you may have, and make a cover for the top using your favorite sewing method. Decorate the fabric with a wreath of folded roses and prairie point leaves. A ring of flower trim surrounds the roses, while a bow made from bias-cut silk cording finishes the wreath.

You Will Need

1 square basket, 12" x 12"

2 squares dupioni silk, 13" x 13"

1 square batting, 13" x 13", ¼" thin

120" cinnamon/raspberry ombre wire-edge ribbon, 1" wide

54" cinnamon/raspberry ombre wire-edge ribbon, 1½" wide

36" raspberry stripe wire-edge ribbon, 1" wide

36" pink ombre wire-edge ribbon, 1" wide

24" green stripe wire-edge ribbon, 1½" wide

28" of pink flower trim

18" olive green bias-cut silk cording, ¼" wide

1 circle crinoline, 7" diameter

Steps

Diagrams are found in Chapter 6 — Techniques Guide.
Basket Cover

1. Cover the basket top using the fabric and batting. Sew the batting to one piece of the fabric. With right sides together, sew the two pieces of fabric together, leaving an opening to turn the piece right side out.

2. Trim the corners, and turn the piece right side out. Slipstitch the opening closed.

Flowers and Leaves

1. Make nine folded roses using the folded rose technique; see diagrams 52 through 57. Make three of the roses using 18" of 1½"-wide cinnamon/raspberry ombre wire-edge ribbon per flower. Make three more roses using 12" of 1"-wide pink ombre wire-edge ribbon per flower. Make the remaining three roses using 12" of 1"-wide raspberry stripe wire-edge ribbon per flower.

2. Make six prairie point leaves using 4" of 1½"-wide green stripe wire-edge ribbon per leaf and the prairie point technique; see diagrams 79 through 82.

3. Sew the roses to the crinoline using the photo as a guide.

4. Evenly arrange and sew the leaves under the roses.

Putting It All Together

1. Sew the flower trim in gentle loops on the outside edge of the rose wreath.

2. Make a shoelace bow, and sew it to the bottom of the wreath, tacking the streamers to the fabric.

3. Cut away all of the exposed crinoline, and sew the wreath composition to the top of the fabric.

4. Make four shoelace bows using 20" of 1"-wide cinnamon/raspberry ombre wire-edge ribbon for each bow. Sew these bows to the corners of the fabric cover.

5. Cut the remaining 1"-wide cinnamon/raspberry ribbon into two 20" lengths. Fold each length in half, and sew the center of the ribbon to the center of two sides of the fabric cover. These will act as ties and may be tied into bows around the basket handle.

Simple
Silk Roses

Silk ribbon roses made using the coil rose and folded rose techniques add grace and sophistication to a wire box.

I nspired by roses in a summer garden, these beautiful — and easy — silk flowers are perfect for a box or a pillow, or singly in a topiary. Here's a great chance to use up gorgeous hand-dyed silk ribbons in your stash.

You Will Need

36" yellow silk embroidery ribbon, 1½" wide
36" taupe silk embroidery ribbon, 1½" wide
36" mauve silk embroidery ribbon, 1½" wide
72" pink/taupe silk embroidery ribbon, 1½" wide
72" pink/yellow silk embroidery ribbon, 1½" wide
1 crinoline oval, 5" x 4"
2 crinoline circles, 2" in diameter

Steps

Diagrams are found in Chapter 6 — Techniques Guide.
Flowers
1. Make five folded roses using 36" of ribbon for each rose — yellow, pink/yellow, taupe, pink/taupe and mauve. Refer to the folded rose technique diagrams; see diagrams 52 through 57.

2. Make two upright coil roses using 36" of ribbon for each rose — pink/taupe and pink/yellow. Refer to the upright coil rose technique; see diagrams 29 through 32. After gathering each rose, sew the center to a 2" circle of crinoline and spiral the gathering around the center until a rose is formed. Sew the "coiled" layers to the crinoline.

Putting It All Together
1. Using the photo as a guide, sew each rose to the crinoline oval. Trim the excess crinoline.

2. Attach the crinoline composition of roses to a box, pillow or project of your choice.

Wooden Jewelry Box
with Roses

Dainty folded roses and leaves
adorn a small wooden jewelry box.

This small wooden box, decorated on top with a few ribbon flowers, is a lovely gift. Make one for yourself and one to give! The ribbons used measure 1" or less in width, and they are very easily made into pretty flowers.

You Will Need

1 wooden box with padded fabric top, 4" square
6" sheer gold edge ribbon, ⅝" wide
9" pink ombre wire-edge ribbon, 1" wide
9" cream wire-edge ribbon, 1" wide
9" pale pink ribbon, 1" wide
6¾" green ruffle-edge ribbon, ¼" wide
18" olive green ombre wire-edge ribbon, 1" wide
18" pink/green flower bud trim
1 crinoline square, 2" x 2"
3 gold seed beads

Steps

Diagrams are found in Chapter 6 — Techniques Guide.
Flowers and Leaves
1. Make a rosette using 6" of ⅜"-wide sheer gold-edge ribbon and the U-gather technique; see diagrams 21 through 23. Sew three gold seed beads to the center.

2. Make three folded roses using 9" of ribbon for each rose — pale pink, pink and cream. Refer to the folded rose technique; see diagrams 52 through 57.

3. Make six prairie point leaves using 3" of 1"-wide olive green wire-edge ribbon per leaf and the prairie point technique; see diagrams 79 through 82.

4. Make six curve leaves using 2¼" of ¼"-wide green ruffle-edge ribbon per leaf and the curve leaf technique; see diagrams 87 through 90.

Putting It All Together
1. Sew or lightly glue the pink rosebud trim around the box edge. Cut the remaining trim into three equal pieces to use in the flower composition.

2. Using the photo as a guide, sew the three roses to the center of the crinoline. Sew the sheer rosette in the center of the three roses.

3. Evenly arrange the prairie point leaves around the roses, and sew them in place. Sew the curve leaves between the other leaves. Sew the small pieces of flower bud trim in and around the leaves.

4. Trim the excess crinoline from the composition, and sew the composition to the box top.

Anniversary Photo Album

Photo albums make great surfaces for ribbonwork.
This album used silk fabrics, ribbon roses and leaves, pleated ribbon
and colorful flower bud trim. Antique album, circa 1890.

A photo album makes a wonderful gift for a special event, such as a golden wedding anniversary. Choose any style of album, and make a fabric print of the recipients to use on the cover. Embellish the fabric cover with ribbon flowers and pretty trims. This post-and-board album features folded roses and buds, fancy rosettes, prairie point leaves and half-boat leaves.

You Will Need

1 post-and-board album, 10" x 11½" cover size
1 fabric print image, at least 5¼" x 3¾"
2 pieces thin cotton batting, 5¼" x 3¾"
2 pieces thin cotton batting, 10" x 11½"
2 squares gold dupioni silk fabric, 14" x 14"
2 sheets coordinating decorative paper
26" dark gold pleated crepe georgette ribbon, ⅝" wide
6" light gold pleated crepe georgette ribbon, ⅝" wide
19" cranberry striped ombre wire-edge ribbon, 1" wide
15" purple striped ombre wire-edge ribbon, 1" wide
5½" pale gold double-face silk satin ribbon, ⅜" wide
5½" beige double-face silk satin ribbon, ⅜" wide
4" olive green ombre wire-edge ribbon, ⅝" wide
12" olive green ombre wire-edge ribbon, 1½" wide
12" green jacquard ribbon, ¾" wide
36" of olive/gold leaf trim
19" multicolored flower bud trim
1 crinoline rectangle, 5" x 4"
Gold seed beads (optional)

Steps

Diagrams are found in Chapter 6 — Techniques Guide.
Album Cover

1. Glue a piece of batting to each album cover. Set one cover aside to be the front cover.

2. With one piece of the gold silk fabric, cover the back album cover, mitering the corners. Finish the inside of the cover with a piece of the decorative paper.

3. Place a piece of batting under fabric print of your choice, and fold the raw edges of the fabric over the batting. Using small running stitches, sew the dark gold pleated crepe ribbon around the print. Set aside.

4. On the remaining piece of gold silk fabric, determine where the fabric print will be placed, and mark it with pins. Measuring from the center of the print, evenly space and stitch in place the olive/gold leaf trim to the fabric to create a striped effect; avoid placing any trim under the area where the photo will be placed. If desired, accent the trim with gold seed beads.

5. Sew the fabric print to the "striped" fabric; at the same time, attach the multicolored flower trim. If desired, accent the print with gold seed beads.

Flowers and Leaves

1. Make two large folded roses, one using 12" of 1"-wide purple striped ombre wire-edge ribbon and one using 12" of 1"-wide cranberry striped ombre wire-edge ribbon. Refer to the folded rose technique; see diagrams 52 through 57.

2. Make one small folded rose using 4" of 1"-wide cranberry striped ombre wire-edge ribbon. Refer to the folded rose technique; see diagrams 52 through 57.

3. Make two basic flat buds, one using 3" of 1"-wide purple striped ombre wire-edge ribbon and one using 3" of 1"-wide cranberry striped ombre wire-edge ribbon. Refer to the basic flat bud technique; see diagrams 42 through 45. Make a calyx for each bud using 2" of ⅝"-wide olive green ombre wire-edge ribbon per bud. Wrap the ribbon around the raw edges, and secure it in the back of the bud with a few stitches.

4. Make two gold roses. The roses are made in two parts — a folded rose for the center and a rosette for the outer ruffle. Make one folded rose center using

5½" of ⅜"-wide pale gold double-face silk satin ribbon and one using 5½" of ⅜"-wide beige double-face silk satin ribbon. Refer to the folded rose technique; see diagrams 52 through 57. Make the outer ruffle using 6" of ⅝"-wide pleated crepe georgette ribbon per ruffle and the U-gather technique; see diagrams 21 through 23. Make one light gold ruffle and one dark gold ruffle. Leave a small hole at the center of the rosette ruffle so the folded rose can be placed in the ruffle. Insert the pale gold folded rose into the center of the light gold rosette, and secure the two together with a few stitches at the center. Insert the beige folded rose into the center of the dark gold rosette. Trim the excess ribbon from the underside of the flower.

5. Make three prairie point leaves using 4" of 1½"-wide olive green ombre wire-edge ribbon per leaf and the prairie point leaf technique; see diagrams 79 through 82.

6. Make three curve leaves using 4" of ¾"-wide green jacquard ribbon per leaf and the curve leaf technique; see diagrams 87 through 90.

Putting It All Together

1. Using the photo as a guide, sew the flowers and leaves to a 5" x 4" piece of crinoline; arrange the design in an L-shaped pattern. Sew the large folded roses first, then add the gold roses, followed by the large leaves. Add the smaller roses and buds last. Cut away the excess crinoline.

2. Sew the composition to the bottom left corner of the fabric print and gold silk fabric.

3. Place the embellished gold silk fabric over the remaining album cover, and finish the front cover as you did for the back cover.

Ornamental Tassels

*Tassels such as these are wonderful to hang on
cabinet doors, light fixtures and ceiling fans.
They also make nice ornaments for Christmas trees.*

Tassels add a tasteful accent to your projects and your home, and they are easy to make. Following are the base "recipes" to prepare fringe tassels and knotted ribbon loop tassels, along with ideas for embellishing.

The Fringe Tassel is the most common type of tassel. You can leave it plain or create a "skirt" of knotted ribbon loops around it, or add beads, lace, ribbon roses, bows or feathers.

The Knotted Ribbon Loop Tassel uses knotted loops of ribbon. For a very festive tassel, select a variety of colorful ribbons and a few pieces of metallic gold eyelash yarn to add interest.

Decorate fringe or knotted ribbon loop tassels with Venice lace, bows, ribbon roses and leaves. Add strands of beads or wispy feathers. The combinations are endless.

Fringe Tassel

You Will Need

9" off-white rayon fringing, 6" deep
6" double-face silk satin ribbon, ⅛" wide
Water
Tea, coffee or silk and rayon dye
Glass or plastic bowl
Paper towel
Craft glue

Steps

1. Decide how thick you want the tassel to be; a length of fringing between 6" and 9" works well.

2. Wet the fringing with water, and immerse it into a dye bath of tea, coffee or dye made for silk and rayon. Remove the fringing when the color is what you like. Gently squeeze out the excess moisture from the fringing, and lay it on a paper towel to dry.

3. Fold a 6" piece of ⅛"-wide silk satin ribbon in half to form a loop hanger. Place it at one end of the fringing with the loop hanger above the fringing band. Smear a very thin layer of craft glue across the top of the fringing. Starting at the loop hanger end, tightly roll up the fringing so the loop hanger will be in the center of the tassel when completed.

Knotted Ribbon Loop Tassel

You Will Need

72" each ribbon in six different colors, ¼" to ½" wide
6" double-face silk satin ribbon, ⅛" wide
Craft glue

Steps

Diagrams are found in Chapter 6 — Techniques Guide.

1. Cut each ribbon into 12" lengths to yield six lengths per color, for a total of 36 pieces.

2. Tie a knot in the center of each ribbon. See diagram 6, and only tie the knot; don't make the loop. Keep the ribbons in their color groups.

3. Take a knotted ribbon from the first group, and fold it into a loop. Secure the thread into the base of the ribbon loop with several backstitches.

4. Take a second knotted ribbon from another group and fold it into a loop. Sew the base of that loop with two tiny running stitches sliding it next to the first loop.

5. Repeat Steps 3 and 4 until you have sewn one of each of the six different ribbons onto the thread. To get a mental image of the loops hanging on the thread, picture laundry hanging on a clothesline.

6. Repeat the sequence of ribbons in Steps 3, 4 and 5 until all of the knotted ribbons have been used.

7. Gather the ribbon loops to about 6", and tightly secure the gathering. Cut the thread. You have now completed the ribbon loop fringing needed to make the tassel.

8. Fold a 6" piece of ⅛"-wide silk satin ribbon in half to form a loop hanger. Place it at one end of the ribbon loop fringing, with the loop hanger above the fringed ribbon band. Smear a very thin layer of glue across the top of the ribbon fringing. Starting at the loop hanger end, tightly roll up the ribbon fringing so the loop hanger will be in the center of the tassel when completed.

Tassel Embellishments

Pink Loop Tassel with Rosettes and Feathers

You Will Need

1 ribbon loop tassel
Fine feathers
7" embroidered lace, 1½" wide
28" hand-dyed silk ribbon, 1½" wide
4 pearl buttons

Steps

Diagrams are found in Chapter 6 — Techniques Guide.
1. Glue several small clusters of fine feathers around a ribbon loop tassel.

2. Make a lace ruffle using 7" of 1½"-wide embroidered lace. Sew the raw edges together in a seam so a tube shape is formed, then gather around the top of the lace. Slip this ruffle over the top of the tassel, and sew or glue it in place.

3. Make four double rosettes using 7" of 1½"-wide hand-dyed silk ribbon and the two-thirds fold-up edge technique; see diagrams 33 through 35. Sew a pearl button to the center of each flower. Sew the four flowers to the top of the tassel.

Alternate Design Idea

Mix different colors of ribbon and metallic trim to make the loops for the tassel. Tip: Thread beads to some of the loops before making a tassel. Tie a festive shoelace bow, and stitch it to the top of the tassel. Cover the center of the bow with a button.

Pink Fringe Tassel
with Cream Bow, Lace and Roses

You Will Need

1 fringe tassel
27" pink pleated crepe georgette ribbon, ⅝" wide
9" Venice lace
18" creamy pink bias-cut silk satin ribbon, 1" wide
12" green/yellow ruffle-edge ribbon, ¼" wide
2 flower beads

Steps

Diagrams are found in Chapter 6 — Techniques Guide.

1. Sew a piece of Venice lace around a fringe tassel.

2. Using 18" of 1"-wide creamy pink bias-cut silk satin ribbon, tie a simple shoelace bow around the top of the tassel.

3. Make three upright coil roses using 9" of ⅝"-wide pink pleated crepe georgette ribbon per flower and the upright coil rose technique; see diagrams 29 through 32. Sew the roses to the bow.

4. Make six curve leaves using 2" of ¼"-wide green/yellow ruffle-edge ribbon and the curve leaf technique; see diagrams 87 through 90. Sew these leaves to the bow and the lace.

5. Sew two flower beads over two of the leaves.

Alternate Design Idea

Mix different colors of ribbon to make the loops for a skirt to go around a fringe tassel. Tie a shoelace bow, and stitch it to the top of the tassel. Make four folded roses, and attach them above the bow.

Lampshade

An elegant lampshade is dressed up with three vintage petal roses, blossoms and leaves. The flowers are sewn to crinoline and stitched to the lampshade.

A silk-covered lampshade is a perfect place to add a composition of ribbon flowers. This grouping of flowers is made up of vintage petal roses, blossoms, rosettes and three styles of leaves. Make as many flowers as you like to cover your lampshades. These flowers would look equally good on a jacket, a hat, purse or pillow. The choices are endless!

You Will Need

36" pink over-dyed ribbon, 1½" wide

7" pink over-dyed ribbon, ⅝" wide

8" pink ombre wire-edge ribbon, 1" wide

12" pink ombre wire-edge ribbon, ⅝" wide

10" raspberry/cinnamon ombre wire-edge ribbon, 1" wide

6" pale peach double-face silk satin ribbon, 1" wide

36½" pink double-face silk satin ribbon, 1" wide

15" blue ribbon, ⅝" wide

5" yellow ribbon, ⅝" wide

11¼" lavender/green ruffle-edge ribbon, ¼" wide

12" green over-dyed ribbon, 1½" wide

24" olive green wire-edge ribbon, 1" wide

24" dark green shirred ribbon, ½" wide

24 white/yellow stamens

1 rectangle crinoline, 9" x 7"

1 square crinoline, 4" x 4"

2 squares crinoline, 3" x 3"

Steps

Diagrams are found in Chapter 6 — Techniques Guide.
Flowers

1. Make one large vintage petal rose. The rose is made in two parts — a folded rose center surrounded by 12 double side-roll petals — and is sewn to a 4" square of crinoline. Make a folded rose for the center using 10" of 1"-wide raspberry/cinnamon wire-edge ribbon and the folded rose technique; see diagrams 52 through 57. Make 12 double side-roll petals using 3" of 1½"-wide pink over-dyed ribbon, and the double side-roll petal technique; see diagrams 73 through 78. The front side of the petal is the side with the rolls. In the center of the crinoline draw a 1¼"-diameter circle. Overlap and sew eight petals (with rolled edges facing you) around the drawn circle. Start a second row by sewing two petals just inside the drawn circle. Sew the folded rose on top of these petals. Overlap and sew two more petals to the front of the folded rose, making sure that the raw edges of the petals are folded under and don't show.

2. Make two small vintage roses. They are made exactly the same way as the large rose, except they are sewn to a 3" circle of crinoline. Draw a ¾"-diameter circle in the center of the crinoline. Make one rose in mixed pinks and peach. Use 6" of ⅝"-wide pink ombre wire-edge ribbon for the center folded rose. Make 12 double side-roll petals from different colored ribbons—four petals using 2" of 1"-wide pink ombre wire-edge ribbon per petal, five petals using 2" of 1"-wide pink double-face silk satin ribbon per petal, and three petals using 2" of 1"-wide pale peach double-face silk satin ribbon per petal. Make one rose in pink exactly the same as the previous rose, except it has 13 petals. Use 6" of ⅝"-wide pink ombre wire-edge ribbon for the folded rose center. Make 12 double side-roll petals using 2" of 1"-wide pink double-face silk satin ribbon per petal, and make a 13th larger petal using 2½" of 1"-wide pink double-face silk satin ribbon. Add the 13th petal over the two petals that cover the folded rose.

3. Make one upright coil rose using 7" of ⅝"-wide pink over-dyed ribbon and the upright coil rose technique; see diagrams 29 through 32.

4. Make four blossoms. Make three using 5" of ⅝"-wide blue ribbon per flower and one using 5" of ⅝"-wide yellow ribbon. Refer to the four-petal U-gather technique; see diagrams 40 through 41. Make a stamen bundle for each flower using six white/yellow stamens per flower, see diagrams 1 and 2.

5. Make five rosettes using 2¼" of ¼" wide lavender/green ruffle-edge ribbon per flower and the U-gather technique; see diagrams 21 through 23 and 26. Sew one gold seed bead in the center of each rosette.

Leaves

1. Make eight small curve leaves using 3" of ½"-wide dark green shirred ribbon per leaf and the curve leaf technique; see diagrams 87 through 90.

2. Make four large curve leaves using 6" of 1"-wide olive green wire-edge ribbon and the curve leaf technique; see diagrams 87 through 90.

3. Make three crossover leaves using 4" of 1½"-wide green over-dyed ribbon and the crossover leaf technique; see diagrams 83 through 85.

Putting It All Together

1. Using the photo as a guide, stitch the large rose and the two smaller roses onto a 9" x 7" piece of crinoline. Only sew the flowers at the center so that the leaves and other elements can be stitched under them.

2. Stitch the large leaves, then the smaller leaves. The small coil rose, blossoms and rosettes are stitched over the leaves and main flowers.

3. After everything has been stitched on, tack down the leaves at their points, and tack down the rose petals about halfway up each petal.

4. Cut away the excess crinoline, and sew the piece to the lampshade. If the shade can't be sewn, then use a very light coat of craft glue to adhere the composition to the shade.

Four Seasons Bell Pull

Decorated fabric bell pulls often were found in parlors and bedrooms in houses from the 18th century through the early 20th century. Bell pulls were attached to a wire or cord on a wall, and, when pulled, caused a small bell to ring in the servants' quarters.

Covered in a myriad of ribbon flowers that are very simple to accomplish, this beautiful bell pull project features a young woman in a garden during spring (shown at left), summer (page 81), autumn (page 83) and winter (page 85). You may choose to make the entire bell pull (shown on page 88) or just one of the seasons. With more than 45 ribbons used to make the flowers, a supply list for the entire project is on page 88; a ribbon-only supply list is also provided for each season. The finished bell pull size is approximately 29" long by 4" wide.

Take your time with this project, and enjoy the passing of the seasons.

Ribbons for Spring Flowers

9" pink over-dyed ribbon, ½" wide

6" pink/white ruffle-edge ribbon, ⅝" wide

24" creamy pink bias-cut silk ribbon, ⅝" wide

8" dark mauve bias-cut silk ribbon, ⅝" wide

6" cream over-dyed silk embroidery ribbon, 13 mm wide

6" palest pink over-dyed silk embroidery ribbon, 13 mm wide

6" palest peach over-dyed silk embroidery ribbon, 13 mm wide

6" palest pink over-dyed silk embroidery ribbon, 7 mm wide

2¼" lavender ruffle-edge ribbon, ¼" wide

4½" pale peach ruffled gold edge ribbon, ¼" wide

2¼" mauve/cream picot-edge ribbon, ¼" wide

Ribbons for Spring Leaves

3¾" olive green leaf trim

4" lime/yellow ombre wire-edge ribbon, ⅝" wide

4" pink/green ombre wire-edge ribbon, ⅝" wide

2" olive pleated crepe georgette ribbon, ⅝" wide

7½" blue/green double-faced silk satin ribbon, ⅜" wide

5¼" yellow/green ruffle-edge ribbon, ¼" wide

Steps

Diagrams are found in Chapter 6 — Techniques Guide.

Spring Flowers

There are 14 flowers in the main composition that are made using three techniques.

1. Make nine ribbon candy roses as follows: three using 8" of ⅝"-wide creamy pink bias-cut silk ribbon per flower (set aside one for the center of the large pink/white rosette); one using 8" of ⅝"-wide dark mauve bias-cut silk ribbon, one using 6" of 13 mm-wide cream over-dyed silk embroidery ribbon, one using 6" of 13 mm-wide palest pink over-dyed silk embroidery ribbon, one using 6" of 13 mm-wide palest peach over-dyed silk embroidery ribbon and two using 6" of 7 mm-wide palest pink over-dyed silk embroidery ribbon per flower. Refer to the ribbon candy rose technique; see diagrams 8 through 10. Sew one to three seed beads to the center of each rose.

2. Make five rosettes as follows: two using 2¼" of ¼"-wide peach ruffled gold edge ribbon per flower, one using 2¼" of ¼"-wide lavender ruffle-edge ribbon, one using 2¼" of ¼"-wide mauve/cream picot-edge ribbon and one using 6" of ⅝"-wide pink/white ruffle-edge ribbon (sew one creamy pink bias-cut ribbon candy rose to the center of this rosette). Refer to the single U-gather technique; see diagrams 21 through 23 and 26. Sew one to three seed beads to the center of each rosette.

3. Make one vintage flat rose using 9" of ½"-wide pink over-dyed ribbon and the vintage flat rose technique; see diagrams 46 through 51. Make the rose on a 1½" square of crinoline and trim away the excess crinoline.

Spring Leaves

There are 11 leaves in the main composition that are made using made three techniques.

1. Make four prairie point leaves — two using 2" of ⅝"-wide lime/yellow ombre wire-edge ribbon per leaf and two using 2" of ⅝"-wide pink/green ombre wire-edge ribbon per leaf. Refer to the prairie point leaf technique; see diagrams 79 through 82.

2. Make six curve leaves — three using 2½" of ⅜"-wide blue-green silk double-faced satin ribbon per leaf and three using 1¾" of ¼"-wide yellow-green ruffle-edge ribbon per leaf. Refer to the curve leaf technique; see diagrams 87 through 90.

3. Make one half-round leaf using 2" of ⅝"-wide olive pleated crepe georgette ribbon and the half-round leaf technique; see diagram 86, and look at diagram 25.

Summer

Ribbons for Summer Flowers
9" blue over-dyed ribbon, ½" wide
5" pink over-dyed ribbon, ½" wide
5" yellow ruffle-edge ribbon, ½" wide
8" creamy pink bias-cut silk ribbon, ⅝" wide
8" dark mauve bias-cut silk ribbon, ⅝" wide
8" apricot bias-cut silk ribbon, ⅝" wide
5" ivory bias-cut silk ribbon, ⁷⁄₁₆" wide
5" pale pink bias-cut silk ribbon, ⁷⁄₁₆" wide
5" dark mauve bias-cut silk ribbon, ⁷⁄₁₆" wide
5" peach/yellow bias-cut silk ribbon, ⁷⁄₁₆" wide
6" palest blush over-dyed silk embroidery ribbon,
   13 mm wide
3" rose silk embroidery ribbon, 7 mm wide
3" palest peach over-dyed silk embroidery ribbon,
   7 mm wide
3" palest yellow over-dyed silk embroidery ribbon,
   7 mm wide
6" pale apricot/yellow silk embroidery ribbon,
   7 mm wide
2¼" blue/green ruffle-edge ribbon, ¼" wide
2¼" lavender ruffle-edge ribbon, ¼" wide
2¼" pink ruffle-edge ribbon, ¼" wide

Ribbons for Summer Leaves
3¾" olive green leaf trim
4" lime/yellow ombre wire-edge ribbon, ⅝" wide
4" olive ombre wire-edge ribbon, ⅝" wide
2" olive pleated crepe georgette ribbon, ⅝" wide
5" dark olive double-faced silk satin ribbon,
   ⅜" wide
5¼" yellow/green ruffle-edge ribbon, ¼" wide

Steps

Diagrams are found in Chapter 6 — Techniques Guide.

Summer Flowers

There are 14 flowers in the main composition and three small ones on the vine that are made using three techniques.

Main Composition

1. Make 10 ribbon candy roses as follows: one using 8" of ⅝"-wide creamy pink bias-cut silk ribbon; one using 8" of ⅝"-wide wide dark mauve bias-cut silk ribbon; one using 8" of ⅝"-wide wide apricot bias-cut silk ribbon; one using 5" of ⁷/₁₆"-wide dark mauve bias-cut silk ribbon; one using 5" of ⁷/₁₆"-wide wide peach/yellow bias-cut silk ribbon; one using 5" of ⁷/₁₆"-wide ivory bias-cut silk ribbon; one using 5" of ⁷/₁₆"-wide pale pink bias-cut silk ribbon; one using 6" of 13 mm-wide palest blush over-dyed silk embroidery ribbon; one using 3" of 7 mm-wide pale apricot/yellow silk embroidery ribbon (set aside for the center of the large yellow rosette); and one using 3" of 7 mm-wide rose over-dyed silk embroidery ribbon. Refer to the ribbon candy rose technique; see diagrams 8 through 10. Sew one to three seed beads to the center of each rose.

2. Make five rosettes as follows: one using 2¼" of ¼"-wide blue/green ruffle-edge ribbon; one using 2¼" of ¼"-wide lavender ruffle-edge ribbon; one using 2¼" of ¼"-wide pink ruffle-edge ribbon (set aside and use as the center for the large pink over-dyed rosette); one using 5" of ½"-wide pink over-dyed ribbon (use the small pink ruffle-edge rosette in the center of this flower); and one using 5" of ½"-wide yellow ruffle-edge ribbon (sew the small apricot/yellow ribbon candy rose to the center of this rosette). Refer to the single U-gather technique; see diagrams 21 through 23 and 26. Sew one to three seed beads to the center of each rosette.

3. Make one vintage flat rose using 9" of ½"-wide blue over-dyed ribbon and the vintage flat rose technique; see diagrams 46 through 51. Make the rose on a 1½" square of crinoline and trim away excess crinoline.

Vine

1. Make three small ribbon candy roses — one using 3" of 7 mm-wide palest yellow over-dyed silk embroidery ribbon; one using 3" of 7 mm-wide pale apricot/yellow silk embroidery ribbon; and one using 3" of 7 mm-wide palest peach over-dyed silk embroidery ribbon. Refer to the ribbon candy rose technique; see diagrams 8 through 10. Sew one seed bead to the center of each rose.

Summer Leaves

There are 10 leaves in the main composition that are made using three techniques.

1. Make four prairie point leaves — two using 2" of ⅝"-wide lime/yellow ombre wire-edge ribbon per leaf and two using 2" of ⅝"-wide olive ombre wire-edge ribbon per leaf. Refer to the prairie point leaf technique; see diagrams 79 through 82.

2. Make five curve leaves — two using 2½" of ⅜"-wide dark olive double-faced silk satin ribbon per leaf; three using 1¾" of ¼"-wide yellow/green ruffle-edge ribbon per leaf. Refer to the curve leaf technique; see diagrams 87 through 90.

3. Make one half-round leaf using 2" of ⅝"-wide olive pleated crepe georgette ribbon and the half-round leaf technique; see diagram 86, and look at diagram 25.

Autumn

Ribbons for Autumn Flowers

9" pink over-dyed ribbon, ½" wide

6" dark gold pleated crepe georgette ribbon, ⅝" wide

8" dark ivory bias-cut silk ribbon, ⅝" wide

8" dark yellow bias-cut silk ribbon, ⅝" wide

8" apricot bias-cut silk ribbon, ⅝" wide

8" pale pink bias-cut silk ribbon, ⅝" wide

10" raspberry/yellow bias-cut silk ribbon, $7/16$" wide

10" peach/yellow bias-cut silk ribbon, $7/16$" wide

3" rose silk embroidery ribbon, 7 mm wide

3" pale apricot/yellow silk embroidery ribbon, 7 mm wide

3" palest peach over-dyed silk embroidery ribbon, 7 mm wide

2¼" blue/green ruffle-edge ribbon, ¼" wide

2¼" lavender ruffle-edge ribbon, ¼" wide

2¼" yellow/pink ruffle-edge ribbon, ¼" wide

4½" red/peach picot-edge ribbon, ¼" wide

Ribbons for Autumn Leaves

3¾" olive green leaf trim

4" wide lime/yellow ombre wire-edge ribbon, ⅝" wide

4" olive ombre wire-edge ribbon, ⅝" wide

2" olive pleated crepe georgette ribbon, ⅝" wide

7½" dark olive double-faced silk satin ribbon, ⅜" wide

5¼" yellow/green ruffle-edge ribbon, ¼" wide

Steps

Diagrams are found in Chapter 6 — Techniques Guide.

Autumn Flowers

There are 14 flowers in the main composition and three small ones on the vine that are made using three techniques.

Main Composition

1. Make eight ribbon candy roses as follows: one using 8" of ⅝"-wide pale pink bias-cut silk ribbon; one using 8" of ⅝"-wide dark yellow bias-cut silk ribbon; one using 8" of ⅝"-wide apricot bias-cut silk ribbon; one using 8" of ⅝"-wide dark ivory bias-cut silk ribbon (set aside and use in the center of the dark gold pleated crepe georgette rosette); two using 5" of 7/16"-wide raspberry/yellow bias-cut silk ribbon per flower; and two using 5" of 7/16"-wide peach/yellow bias-cut silk ribbon per flower. Refer to the ribbon candy rose technique; see diagrams 8 through 10. Sew one to three seed beads to the center of each rose.

2. Make six rosettes as follows: one using 2¼" of ¼"-wide blue/green ruffle-edge ribbon; one using 2¼" of ¼"-wide lavender ruffle-edge ribbon; one using 2¼" of ¼"-wide yellow/pink ruffle-edge ribbon; two rosettes using 2¼" of ¼"-wide red/peach picot-edge ribbon per flower; and one using 6" of 5/8"-wide dark gold pleated crepe georgette (sew the large dark ivory ribbon candy rose to the center of this rosette). Refer to the single U-gather technique; see diagrams 21 through 23 and 26. Sew one to three seed beads to the center of each rosette.

3. Make one vintage flat rose using 9" of ½"-wide pink over-dyed ribbon and the vintage flat rose technique; see diagrams 46 through 51. Make the rose on a 1½" square of crinoline, and trim away the excess crinoline.

Vine

1. Make three small ribbon candy roses — one using 3" of 7 mm-wide palest peach over-dyed silk embroidery ribbon; one using 3" of 7 mm-wide pale apricot/yellow silk embroidery ribbon; and one using 3" of 7 mm-wide rose silk embroidery ribbon. Refer to the ribbon candy rose technique; see diagrams 8 through 10. Sew one seed bead to the center of each rose.

Autumn Leaves

There are 11 leaves in the main composition that are made using three techniques.

1. Make four prairie point leaves — two using 2" of 5/8"-wide lime/yellow ombre wire-edge ribbon per leaf; and two using 2" of 5/8"-wide olive ombre wire-edge ribbon per leaf. Refer to the prairie point leaf technique; see diagrams 79 through 82.

2. Make six curve leaves — three using 2½" of 3/8"-wide dark olive double-faced silk satin ribbon per leaf; and three using 1¾" of ¼"-wide yellow/green ruffle-edge ribbon per leaf. Refer to the curve leaf technique; see diagrams 87 through 90.

3. Make one half-round leaf using 2" of 5/8"-wide olive pleated crepe georgette ribbon, and the half-round leaf technique; see diagram 86, and look at diagram 25.

Winter

Ribbons for Winter Flowers

9" blue over-dyed ribbon, ½" wide

5" pumpkin over-dyed ribbon, ½" wide

6" brown picot-edge ribbon, ⅝" wide

8" dark yellow bias-cut silk ribbon, ⅝" wide

16" dark ivory bias-cut silk ribbon, ⅝" wide

10" burgundy/gold bias-cut silk ribbon, ⁷⁄₁₆" wide

5" dark mauve bias-cut silk ribbon, ⁷⁄₁₆" wide

3" rose silk embroidery ribbon, 7 mm wide

3" pale apricot/yellow silk embroidery ribbon,
   7 mm wide

6" medium peach silk embroidery ribbon,
   7 mm wide

6¾" yellow/pink ruffle-edge ribbon, ¼" wide

2¼" blue/green ruffle-edge ribbon, ¼" wide

2¼" mauve/cream picot-edge ribbon, ¼" wide

2¼" apricot/olive picot-edge ribbon, ¼" wide

Ribbons for Winter Leaves

3¾" olive green leaf trim

4" lime/yellow ombre wire-edge ribbon, ⅝" wide

4" olive ombre wire-edge ribbon, ⅝" wide

2" olive pleated crepe georgette ribbon, ⅝" wide

7½" dark olive double-faced silk satin ribbon,
   ⅜" wide

5¼" yellow/green ruffle-edge ribbon, ¼" wide

Steps

Diagrams are found in Chapter 6 — Techniques Guide.

Winter Flowers

There are 14 flowers in the main composition and three small ones on the vine that are made using three techniques.

Main Composition

1. Make seven ribbon candy roses as follows: one using 8" of ⅝"-wide dark yellow bias-cut silk ribbon; two using 8" of ⅝"-wide dark ivory bias-cut silk ribbon per flower; two using 5" of ⁷/₁₆"-wide burgundy/gold bias-cut silk ribbon per flower (sew one of these to the center of the large brown rosette); one using 5" of ⁷/₁₆"-wide dark mauve bias-cut silk ribbon; and one using 6" of 7 mm-wide medium peach silk embroidery ribbon. Refer to the ribbon candy rose technique; see diagrams 8 through 10. Sew one to three seed beads to the center of each rose.

2. Make eight rosettes as follows: one using 2¼" of ¼"-wide blue/green ruffle-edge ribbon; three using 2¼" of ¼"-wide yellow/pink ruffle-edge ribbon per flower (sew one of these rosettes to the center of the large pumpkin rosette); one using 2¼" of ¼"-wide apricot/olive picot-edge ribbon; one using 5" of ½" wide pumpkin over-dyed ribbon (sew one yellow/pink rosette to the center of this rosette); one using 6" of ⅝"-wide brown picot-edge ribbon (sew one small burgundy/gold ribbon candy rose in the center of this rosette); and one using 2¼" of ¼"-wide apricot/olive picot-edge ribbon. Refer to the single U-gather technique; see diagrams 21 through 23 and 26. Sew one to three seed beads to the center of each rosette.

3. Make one vintage flat rose using 9" of ½"-wide blue over-dyed ribbon, and the vintage flat rose technique; see diagrams 46 through 51. Make the rose on a 1½" square of crinoline and trim away the excess crinoline.

Vine

1. Make three small ribbon candy roses — one using 3" of 7 mm-wide medium peach silk embroidery ribbon; one using 3" of 7 mm-wide pale apricot/yellow silk embroidery ribbon; and one using 3" of 7 mm-wide rose silk embroidery ribbon. Refer to the ribbon candy rose technique; see diagrams 8 through 10. Sew one seed bead to the center of each rose.

Winter Leaves

There are 11 leaves in the main composition that are made using three techniques.

1. Make four prairie point leaves — two using 2" of ⅝"-wide lime/yellow ombre wire-edge ribbon per leaf; and two using 2" of ⅝"-wide olive ombre wire-edge ribbon per leaf. Refer to the prairie point leaf technique; see diagrams 79 through 82.

2. Make six curve leaves — three using 2½" of ⅜" wide dark olive double-faced silk satin ribbon per leaf; and three using 1¾" of ¼"-wide yellow/green ruffle-edge ribbon per leaf. Refer to the curve leaf technique; see diagrams 87 through 90.

3. Make one half-round leaf using 2" of ⅝"-wide olive pleated crepe georgette ribbon, and the half-round leaf technique; see diagram 86, and look at diagram 25.

Bell Pull

Steps

Base

1. Make the fabric bell pull base. Fuse interfacing to the back of the silk fabric to stabilize fabric.

2. Sew the lace to the front of the silk fabric.

3. Fuse webbing to the back of the jacquard ribbon, and iron the ribbon to center of the lace/silk fabric.

Putting It All Together

1. Cut an oval of thin padding the size of the image area of the fabric print, and pin it in place on the back of each fabric print. Using a variety of seed bead colors, sew the seed beads to the front of the fabric prints to give dimension to the "garden flowers."

2. Turn the edges of the print under so no white edging shows. Using a needle and thread, gently gather around the oval shape so the white edges are drawn into the back of the print and over the thin batting.

3. Sew the Spring print to the bell pull, leaving 2½" to 3" from the top of the fabric to the top of the fabric print. Sew the other prints to the fabric, leaving approximately 2½" between each print. Sew 8" of gold loop edging to only the areas of the oval print that will show.

4. Using the photo for each season as a guide, sew all of the flowers and leaves around the print. Start with the large flowers and large leaves, and then work in the small flowers and leaves. Everything will overlap. Sew 3¾" of leaf trim in a curve at the top of the silk print so it reaches the underside of the print above. Sew three tiny roses to each vine segment.

5. Make a tassel; refer to Ornamental Tassels for detailed instructions. Tea-dye 6" of off-white fringing and let it dry. When dry, use 6" of ⅛"-wide cream silk satin ribbon to make a loop, and glue it to one end of the fringing. Spread a little glue along the top edge of the fringing. Starting on the end with the ribbon loop, tightly roll it up into a tassel shape. The ribbon loop should now be coming out in the middle of the tassel. As desired, decorate the tassel with strands of beads,

a bee button and a bee tassel topper. Or, simply make extra flowers and put them around the top of the tassel.

6. With right sides together, sew the backing to the front of the bell pull, leaving a gap at the top.

7. Turn the fabric right side out, and gently press the edges. Turn in the top raw edges of the fabric, and whipstitch them closed. Thread the top of the fabric through the bell pull hardware, and slipstitch it to secure it to the rod. Sew the tassel to the bottom of the bell pull.

8. Optional: Add trim such as metallic braid, flower bud trim, ruffle-edge ribbon or lace around the sides of the bell pull.

You Will Need (For the Entire Project)

1 metal bell pull, 4" wide

4 fabric seasonal prints with image area
2¾" wide x 4½" high

2 strips cream dupioni silk fabric, each 31" x 5"

1 rectangle quilt batting, 8" x 10", ¼" thin

1 strip lightweight interfacing, 31" x 5"

1 strip cool-temperature fusible webbing,
31" x 1½"

1 strip embroidered net lace, 31" x 5"

32" metallic gold loop trim

72" metallic braid, ⅝" wide

31" ivory jacquard shirred ribbon, 1⅝" wide

23" pink over-dyed ribbon, ½" wide

18" blue over-dyed ribbon, ½" wide

5" pumpkin over-dyed ribbon, ½" wide

6" brown picot-edge ribbon, ⅝" wide

6" dark gold pleated crepe georgette ribbon,
⅝" wide

6" pink/white ruffle-edge ribbon, ⅝" wide

5" yellow ruffle-edge ribbon, ½" wide

2¼" pink ruffle-edge ribbon, ¼" wide

9" yellow/pink ruffle-edge ribbon, ¼" wide

6¾" lavender ruffle-edge ribbon, ¼" wide

6¾" blue/green ruffle-edge ribbon, ¼" wide

4½" pale peach ruffled gold-edge ribbon,
¼" wide

4½" mauve/cream picot-edge ribbon, ¼" wide

4½" red/peach picot-edge ribbon, ¼" wide

2¼" apricot/olive picot-edge ribbon, ¼" wide

8" pale pink bias-cut silk ribbon, ⅝" wide

24" dark ivory bias-cut silk ribbon, ⅝" wide

16" apricot bias-cut silk ribbon, ⅝" wide

32" creamy pink bias-cut silk ribbon, ⅝" wide

16" dark mauve bias-cut silk ribbon, ⅝" wide

16" dark yellow bias-cut silk ribbon, ⅝" wide

15" peach/yellow bias-cut silk ribbon, ⁷⁄₁₆" wide

10" raspberry/yellow bias-cut silk ribbon,
⁷⁄₁₆" wide

10" burgundy/gold bias-cut silk ribbon,
⁷⁄₁₆" wide

10" dark mauve bias-cut silk ribbon, ⁷⁄₁₆" wide

5" ivory bias-cut silk ribbon, ⁷⁄₁₆" wide

5" apricot bias-cut silk ribbon, ⁷⁄₁₆" wide

5" pale pink bias-cut silk ribbon, ⁷⁄₁₆" wide

6" cream over-dyed silk embroidery ribbon,
13 mm wide

6" palest pink over-dyed silk embroidery ribbon,
13 mm wide

6" palest peach over-dyed silk embroidery
ribbon, 13 mm wide

6" palest blush over-dyed silk embroidery
ribbon, 13 mm wide

3" palest yellow over-dyed silk embroidery
ribbon, 7 mm wide

6" palest pink over-dyed silk embroidery ribbon,
7 mm wide

6" palest peach over-dyed silk embroidery
ribbon, 7 mm wide

9" rose silk embroidery ribbon, 7 mm wide

12" pale apricot/yellow silk embroidery ribbon,
7 mm wide

6" medium peach silk embroidery ribbon,
7 mm wide

16" lime/yellow ombre wire-edge ribbon,
⅝" wide

12" olive ombre wire-edge ribbon, ⅝" wide

4" pink/green ombre wire-edge ribbon,
⅝" wide

7½" blue/green double-faced silk satin ribbon,
⅜" wide

20" dark olive double-faced silk satin ribbon,
⅜" wide

22" yellow/green ruffle-edge ribbon, ¼" wide

8" olive pleated crepe georgette ribbon,
⅝" wide

15" olive green leaf trim

6" cream double-face silk satin ribbon,
⅛" wide

6" off-white tassel fringing, 6" deep

4 squares crinoline, 1½" x 1½"

Assorted seed beads in flower colors
and greens

Assorted seed and small beads in crystal, pearl,
gold and copper

Enamel flower buttons (optional)

Enamel bee and ladybug buttons (optional)

Brass tassel topper (optional)

Elegant Victorian Flowers

*A fabric print and a composition of roses and blossoms
may be used to decorate a Christmas stocking,
a pillow or any other project.*

The focus of this project is the fabric print with the large composition of ribbon flowers around it. The flowers in this project are shown on a stocking made with dupioni silk and vintage metallic laces. If you choose to use this design on a stocking, use your own methods to make a stocking with your own fabrics and laces, or purchase a stocking. Or, perhaps you might like to use this design on a pillow, on a box, on a tote or as a small wall hanging or framed piece.

You Will Need

1 fabric print, image area approximately 2¼" x 3½"

1 piece batting, 2¼" x 3½", ¼" thin

15" peach pink/yellow ombre wire-edge ribbon, 1½" wide

15" nutmeg/yellow ombre wire-edge ribbon, 1½" wide

10" aqua/taupe ombre wire-edge ribbon, 1½" wide

10" blue/green ribbon, ½" wide

10" tan/cream ombre ribbon, ½" wide

5" blue over-dyed ribbon, ½" wide

6¾" red ombre picot-edge ribbon, ¼" wide

9" pink ombre picot-edge ribbon, ¼" wide

12" olive green ombre picot-edge ribbon, ¼" wide

7½" green/brown stripe wire-edge ribbon, 1" wide

10½" olive green over-dyed ribbon, ½" wide

45½" blue/green double-face silk satin ribbon, ⅜" wide

1 crinoline square, 2" x 2"

Seed beads in blue/green, blue, red and gold

Steps

Diagrams are found in Chapter 6 — Techniques Guide.

Fabric Print

1. Place the 2¼" x 3½" piece of batting under the image area of the fabric print. Embellish the print with red seed beads for holly berries. Fold the edges of the fabric print over the batting, and then hand sew the print to the background fabric you are using on your project.

2. Embellish around the fabric print with ruched ribbon, using 33" of ⅜" wide blue/green double-face silk satin ribbon and the zigzag ruching technique; see diagrams 11 and 12.

3. Sew the ruched ribbon around the print with tacking stitches, adding the blue/green seed beads as you go. The join will be hidden by the flower composition.

Flowers

1. Make two cabochon roses — one using 1½"-wide peachy-pink/yellow ombre ribbon and one using 1½"-wide nutmeg/yellow ombre ribbon. If you are using wire-edge ribbon, remove both wires from the ribbon before stitching. The rose is made in two parts: a coil rose center and three outer rolled-edge petals. Make the rose center using use 6" of 1½" wide ombre ribbon per rose and the upright coil rose technique; see diagrams 29 through 32. Before you make the coil rose, fold the ribbon in half so the width becomes ¾" instead of 1½", then follow the diagrams aligning the folded edge of the ribbon at the top of the first diagram. When the rose is made, trim the raw ends from the bottom of the rose. Sew the upright coil rose to a 1" circle of crinoline and set aside. Make three outer petals for each rose using 3" of 1½"-wide ombre ribbon per petal and the rolled edge U-gather technique; see diagrams 36 through 39. Overlap and sew the three rolled-edge petals around the coil rose center.

2. Make five blossoms — two using 5" of ½"-wide tan/cream ombre ribbon per flower; two using 5" of ½"-wide blue/green ribbon per flower; and one using 5" of ½"-wide blue over-dyed ribbon. Refer to the four-petal U-gather technique; see diagrams 40 through 41. Sew seven blue seed beads to the center of each blue flower and seven gold beads to the tan flowers.

3. Make one large rosette using 10" of 1½"-wide aqua/taupe ombre ribbon and the bottom fold two-thirds U-gather technique; see diagrams 33 through 35. Sew nine blue/green seed beads to the center.

4. Make seven small rosettes — three using 2¼" of ¼"-wide red ombre picot-edge ribbon and four using 2¼" of pink ombre picot-edge ribbon. Refer to the U-gather technique; see diagrams 21 through 23 and 26. Sew one gold seed bead to the center of each rosette.

Leaves

1. Make three prairie point leaves using 2½" of 1"-wide green/brown stripe wire-edge ribbon per leaf and the prairie point technique; see diagrams 79 through 82.

2. Make 14 curve leaves — six using 2" of ¼"-wide olive green ombre picot-edge ribbon per leaf; five using 2½" of ⅜"-wide blue/green double-face silk satin ribbon per leaf; and three using 3½" of ½"-wide olive green over-dyed ribbon. Refer to the curve leaf technique; see diagrams 87 through 90.

Putting It All Together

1. Sew the composition directly to the fabric or to the crinoline, depending on the type of project you are making. If you are using crinoline, you will need to cut away the excess crinoline after you've sewn on the flowers and leaves, but before you attach the entire composition to your project. For simplicity, these instructions are for sewing the composition directly to fabric.

2. Using the photo as a guide, sew the two large roses to the fabric.

3. Sew the largest leaves around the roses. Add the large rosette and blossoms, filling in with the smaller leaves and rosettes.

Velvet Brooch Pillow

Small pillows decorated with simple ribbon candy roses and loop leaves may be used as ring pillows, brooch holders and pincushions.

H and-dyed velvet and bias-cut silk ribbons are used to make this sweet little pillow, which can be used at a wedding as a ring bearer pillow, in your sewing room as a pincushion or on your dresser to hold your brooches. Add a pin, antique brooch or beaded stickpin in the pillow top to lend a little sparkle to the project. The techniques to make the roses, leaves and bow are easily mastered.

You Will Need

1 piece pink/mauve hand-dyed silk velvet, 4½" x 9"

24" pale pink bias-cut silk satin ribbon, 1½" wide

54" pink/mauve bias-cut silk ribbon, 7/16" wide

12" pink/mauve bias-cut silk ribbon, 1"-wide

12" pale pink bias-cut silk ribbon, 1" wide

12" creamy pink bias-cut silk ribbon, 1" wide

15" olive green bias-cut silk ribbon, 7/16" wide

1 crinoline rectangle, 1½" x 2"

1 small handful pillow stuffing

1 package pearl seed beads

Steps

Diagrams are found in Chapter 6 — Techniques Guide.

1. Fold the piece of velvet in half, right sides together, to form a square. Sew up two of the sides and partially across the third side, leaving an opening for turning. Turn the pillow right side out. Lightly stuff the pillow, and then sew the opening shut.

2. Ruche 54" of 7/16"-wide pink/mauve bias-cut silk ribbon using the zigzag ruching technique; see diagrams 11 and 12. Gather it to fit around the edge of the pillow. Enhance the edging by sewing pearl seed beads to the ruching as you sew it to the pillow.

3. Make one double-loop bow using 24" of 1½"-wide pale pink bias-cut silk satin ribbon. Cut the ribbon into two 12" lengths. With one piece of ribbon, make two uneven loops (2" tall and 2½" tall), folding the 3" tail back under the two loops. Gather through all of the ribbon layers at the bottom of the loops, and then stitch the "half bow" to the crinoline. Repeat for the second piece of ribbon. Refer to the two-loop bow technique; see diagram 13. The roses will cover the center of the bow.

4. Make three ribbon candy roses using 12" of 1"-wide bias-cut silk ribbon per flower. Make one pale pink, one pink/mauve and one creamy pink. Refer to the ribbon candy rose technique; see diagrams 8 through 10.

5. Make three sets of loop leaves using 5" of 7/16"-wide green bias-cut silk ribbon per set and the two-loop bow technique; see diagram 13. Fan out the loops. Sew one set of loop leaves to the back of each rose.

Putting It All Together

1. Sew three rose/leaf combinations onto the center of the bow so the bow's raw ends are covered.

2. Cut away the excess crinoline, and sew the bow composition to the center of the pillow.

Neck Purse
Name Tag

Make a simple name tag using leftovers from other projects.
Embellish the front with iron-on crystals for a dash of sparkle.

This neck purse/name tag is "Victorian Vegas" at its best! Make it using leftover scraps of Ultrasuede, Venice lace, a fabric print and ribbon flowers, seed beads or crystals. The flowers are a mix of handmade ribbon candy roses and ready-made small flowers. The pocket in the back of the name tag is perfect for storing folding money or a credit card — ready for the next "must-have" ribbon purchase!

You Will Need

1 rectangle Ultrasuede, any color, 3¼" x 9"

1 lady in a hat fabric print rectangle, 3" x 3½"

1 lace appliqué, 3" x 6"

36" pink/olive green loop trim

6" pale yellow ruffle-edge ribbon, ½" wide

16" creamy pink bias-cut silk ribbon, ⅝" wide

8" dusty lavender bias-cut silk ribbon, ⅝" wide

8" apricot bias-cut silk ribbon, ⅝" wide

5" mauve bias-cut silk ribbon, ⁷⁄₁₆" wide

3" palest pink embroidery silk ribbon, 7 mm wide

4½" purple ombre picot-edge ribbon, ¼" wide

2¼" yellow ombre picot-edge ribbon, ¼" wide

3 ready-made roses in red, dusty lavender, mauve

Assorted 2 mm and 3 mm iron-on crystals in crystal and pink

Embroidery floss (optional)

Assorted seed beads in pink, pearl and crystal

Tea

Water

Glass or plastic bowl

Dyes or watered-down acrylic paint in pale green and pink

Paintbrush

Disappearing ink fabric pen

Toothpick

Craft glue

Steps

Diagrams are found in Chapter 6 — Techniques Guide.
Name Tag

1. Cut out the shapes of the lace you wish to use on the project, and discard the rest. Tea dye the lace, and then "paint" the lace shapes in pale green and pink using dyes or watered down acrylic paint. Let the lace dry.

2. Fold the Ultrasuede in half, and sew up the long side seams using a ⅛" seam allowances. Turn the piece right side out. On one edge of the pocket, fold over ½" of Ultrasuede to the inside of the pocket, and glue it in place. This will be the back of the pocket.

3. Fold under the edges of the fabric print so it measures 3" tall by 2½" wide. Embellish the front of the fabric print with two small roses on the hat. Use one ready-made rose, and make a ribbon candy rose using 3" of 7 mm-wide palest pink embroidery silk ribbon and the ribbon candy rose technique; see diagrams 8 through 10. Sew one seed bead to the center of each rose.

4. Using a disappearing ink fabric pen, write in your name, and then embroider it or use iron-on crystals over the markings. You might have to use your initials if you have a long name. Smear a very thin layer of craft glue around the back edges of the print, and adhere it to the front of the pouch, about ¾" up from the bottom fold.

5. Make four ribbon candy roses using 8" of ⅝"-wide bias-cut silk ribbon per flower — one apricot, one dusty lavender and two creamy pink. Make one mauve ribbon candy rose using 5" of ⁷⁄₁₆"-wide mauve bias-cut silk ribbon. Refer to the ribbon candy rose technique; see diagrams 8 through 10. Sew three seed beads in the color of your choice to the center of each rose.

6. Make one yellow upright coil rose using 6" of ½"-wide pale yellow ruffle-edge ribbon and the upright coil rose technique; see diagrams 29 through 32.

7. Make three rosettes — two purple and one yellow — using 2¼" of ¼"-wide picot-edge ribbon. Refer to the U-gather technique; see diagrams 21 through 23 and 26.

8. Add an iron-on crystal or seed bead in the center of each rosette.

Putting It All Together

1. Using the photo as a guide, sew the flowers to the lace shapes. Sew one creamy pink rose, one small mauve rose, one purple rosette and one ready-made red flower to the top piece of lace. Sew one dusty lavender rose, one creamy pink rose, one apricot rose, one yellow rose, one purple rosette, one yellow rosette and one ready-made mauve rose to the bottom piece of lace.

2. Using a toothpick, dot the back of the lace with glue in the areas that will touch the front of the pouch. Adhere the lace to the pouch.

3. Sew or glue the pink/green loop trim along the sides of the pouch to form a neck strap. Cut away the excess Ultrasuede from the top of the pouch.

Elizabeth Half Doll Pincushion

*Small scraps of ribbons, flower trim and fabric are combined
to make a dress and flower bouquet for a sweet little half doll pincushion.*

Ribbonwork and half dolls go hand in hand, as evidenced in the sewing books of the 1920s. These little porcelain half figures — mostly in the shapes of ladies — graced boudoirs, sewing rooms, kitchens and parlors as powder puff toppers, bedside lamps, pincushions, whisk brooms and tea cozies. Sometimes, these half dolls were in the shape of little girls, and they were used most often as pincushions.

You Will Need

2¼" tall half doll – Elizabeth
Pillow stuffing
1 muslin rectangle, 11" long x 5" deep
1 muslin circle, 4" diameter
1 cream silk rectangle, 18" long x 5" deep
1 cream embroidered net lace rectangle,
   18" long x 5" deep
3" lavender/pink ruffle-edge ribbon, ¼" wide
6" pink ruffle-edge ribbon, ¼" wide
18" pale green double-face silk satin ribbon, ⅛" wide
5" multicolored pastel flower trim
8" pink flower bud trim
1 crinoline circle, 1½" diameter
1 butterfly button
Cardboard

Steps

Diagrams are found in Chapter 6 — Techniques Guide.

Pincushion Base

1. Using ½" seam allowances, sew the short sides of the 11" x 5" rectangle of muslin together to form a tube shape. Sew the 4" circle of muslin to the base of the tube, referring to the illustration. Place a circle of cardboard inside the tube at the base. This helps to stabilize the pincushion after it is filled. Tightly pack the tube with pillow stuffing. Gather the top of the tube about ½" to 1" from the edge of the fabric. Tighten and secure the gathering.

2. Sew the half doll to the top of the pincushion using doubled thread through the sew holes on the doll.

Doll's Dress

1. Turn up the edges of the silk fabric by ¼" on each long side and hem. The finished fabric width will now be 4½".

2. Tack the lace to the dress fabric, aligning the bottom of the lace with the bottom of the fabric. Fold over the lace at the top of the "dress" to the underside of the dress. Tack the lace in place at the top of the dress. Make a tube-style skirt by folding the fabric in half and sewing a seam along the short ends of the fabric. Trim the excess lace from the inside of the dress. Turn the dress right side out and gather around the top, but don't tighten it yet.

3. Slip the dress over the doll's head and pincushion base. Tighten the gathering, and secure the dress.

Flowers for the Bouquet

1. Make three miniature upright coil roses using 3" of ¼"-wide ruffle-edge ribbon per flower and the coil rose technique; see diagrams 29 through 32. Make two pale pink roses and one lavender/pink rose. Sew the three roses to a 1½" circle of crinoline. Sew 5" of multicolored pastel flower trim around the three roses. Cut away the excess crinoline. Sew the bouquet to the right side of the doll's skirt, near the waist.

2. Sew a 5" piece of pink rosebud trim down the left side of the doll's dress, starting under her hand. Make two shoelace bows using 9" of ⅛"-wide pale green double-face silk satin ribbon. Sew a bow under each of the doll's hands.

3. Create a wreath using 3" of pink rosebud trim, and glue this to the doll's head.

4. Sew a butterfly button to the right side of the doll's skirt, near the bouquet.

Chapter 6
Techniques Guide

*Four Seasons Bell Pull (summer) featuring vintage flat rose,
ribbon candy rose, rosette, prairie point leaf and curve leaf techniques.*

Stamens

Unstemmed Stamens

Diagram 1

Gather the required amount of stamens needed for a particular flower. Simply wrap some thread around and around the center of the stems, and tie the thread in a knot.

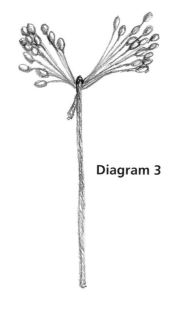

Diagram 1

Diagram 2

Fold the stamens in half, and wrap the folded stamens a few times. Secure them with a knot. Now the stamens are ready to insert into a flower center. Never cut the stamen stems; they will be tucked under a flower or leaf and hidden in the composition.

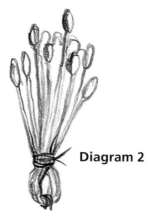

Diagram 2

Stemmed Stamens

Diagram 3

Select enough stamens for the required flower, and wrap the center with thread as in diagram 1. Hook a thread-covered wire around the center of the stamen bundle and over the thread. Twist the wire a few times so it holds the stamens tightly. Use a 2" to 4" piece of 32-gauge wire for small flowers and an 8" to 18" piece of 18-gauge or 20-gauge wire for large flowers.

Diagram 3

Diagram 4

Fold the stamen bundle up, and wrap it with more thread near the base of the wire. The addition of a little glue at the junction of the stems and the wire helps with stability. Now the stem is ready to receive petals, or the stem can be inserted into a smaller flower center.

Diagram 4

Stems and Calyxes

Wired Stem Tips

If a flower doesn't have stamens but still needs a stem, glue or sew an appropriate-sized wire into the first few folds of the ribbon when you are beginning the flower technique. This also applies to stemming leaves.

Cover stems with floral tape or bias-cut silk ribbon. When using bias-cut silk ribbon, smear a very thin layer of craft glue around the base of the petals and down the stem. The ribbon is overlapped as it is wrapped down the stem. A dab of glue at the end of the ribbon will secure it to the base of the stem.

To make a stem seem fatter, slip a length of bias-cut silk cording over the stem, and secure it with a little dab of glue at the junction of the base of the petals and the top of the cording stem cover.

Twisted Ribbon Stem

Diagram 5
Turn under the raw edges, and stitch one end of the ribbon to the crinoline or background fabric. Twist the ribbon in a clockwise motion until the desired length of stem is achieved. Tack the stem in several places using stitches that are hidden in the folds of the ribbon.

Calyx Tips

A calyx covers the raw edges of the flower. For a large or small rose with a wire stem, simply wrap the raw edges of the flower with floral tape or bias-cut silk ribbon, and then proceed down the stem.

For a very small bud, use 1" of ⅜"-wide ribbon (or, if it's a slightly bigger bud, 2" of ½"- wide ribbon), and place it about one-third of the way up the front of the bud. Fold it to the back, and secure it with stitches.

Knotted Loops

Diagram 6
Tie a knot in the center of the ribbon, and overlap the raw ends of the ribbon. Secure the overlap with a few backstitches. If short lengths of ribbon are used, this will make a petal. If a long piece of ribbon is used, it will make a tassel loop. To make a tassel, sew a string of knotted loops together using small running stitches. Smear a thin layer of glue on the sewn edge, and roll it up so a tassel is formed.

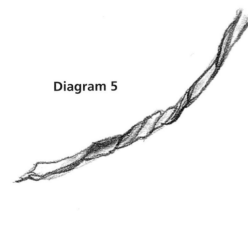

Diagram 5

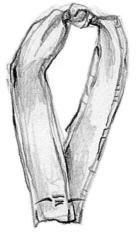

Diagram 6

Ruching Ribbon

Straight Ruching

Diagram 7

Secure your thread in the ribbon with backstitches. Proceed with small, even gathering stitches along the center of the ribbon. Gather the ribbon to the fullness needed for use.

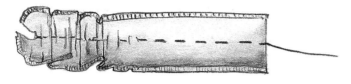

Diagram 7

Ribbon Candy Rose

Diagram 8

Turn in the corners of the raw edges of the ribbon and fold over so an envelope point is formed. Secure the fold with four backstitches. Sew very large stitches along the ribbon; the stitch length is the same size as the width of the ribbon.

Diagram 8

Diagram 9

Gently pull up the gathering so that large folds are formed.

Diagram 9

Diagram 10

Twist the folds so they are not lined up, and then pull the thread very tightly. Secure the thread on the underside of the rose. If desired, sew a seed bead to the center of the rose. Each rose will look different.

Diagram 10

Zigzag Ruching

Diagram 11

Anchor the thread in the ribbon with backstitches, and sew the stitch pattern shown using small running stitches. Think of a right-angle or a 90-degree V-shape every time you come to an edge; then you will have evenly spaced ruching. Be sure the thread goes over the edge of the ribbon each time you make a 90-degree turn.

Diagram 11

Diagram 12

Gather the ribbon to the fullness needed for the project. Secure the gathering with backstitches, and cut the thread. Cut the excess ribbon.

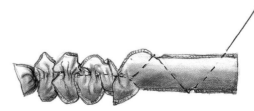

Diagram 12

Loops and Bows

Multiple Loops

Diagram 13

Fold the ribbon into even or uneven loops. If it's required for the project, leave a tail. Secure the folds with stitches at the base. If you are making a looped bow, sew one set of loops to crinoline and another set opposite. Cover the center of the bow with a piece of ribbon so all of the raw edges are covered.

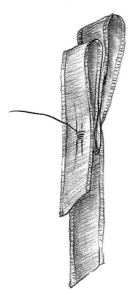

Diagram 13

Diagram 14

Fold the ribbon into loops as required in the project. Sometimes, you will need to leave enough ribbon for a tail. Secure with stitches at the base.

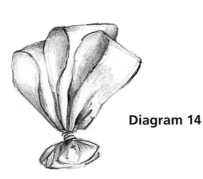

Diagram 14

Figure-Eight Loop Bows

Diagram 15

Fold the ribbon into a loop, and take a small backstitch at the point where the two ribbons overlap. This will become the center of the bow.

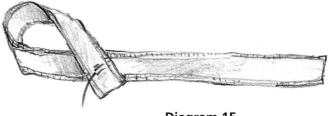

Diagram 15

Diagram 16

Make a second loop opposite the first loop, and secure that loop at the overlap. A small ribbon flower can be sewn over the overlap, as can a button or some beads.

Diagram 16

Tubes

Bell Flower or Lily of the Valley

Diagram 17
Fold the ribbon in half. Your ribbon may look different than the ribbon in the diagram. If the ribbon is ruffled, the ruffle is at the bottom.

Diagram 17

Diagram 18
Begin backstitches ⅛" in from the raw edge; stitch the side seam starting from the bottom and sew toward the top edge. Secure the seam with backstitches at the top. Do not cut the thread.

Diagram 18

Diagram 19
Insert a stem using wire or gimp. If you are using wire, make a small circle in the end of the wire and hook it over the top edge of the ribbon. Stitch around the top of the ribbon tube, and gather it tightly, being sure to catch the stem (sew through the wire circle or through the gimp) when securing the gathering.

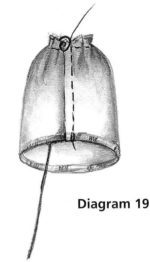

Diagram 19

Diagram 20
Invert the tube. The stem is at the top of the tube, and all of the raw edges are inside. Before stitching near the base of the ribbon, decide how much of a flared look you want. If the ribbon is straight (not ruffled), run a gathering stitch around the tube about one-quarter of the way up from the bottom edge of the ribbon. Gently tighten it so the "petals" flare out. If you are using ruffle-edge ribbon, stitch right at the junction of the straight ribbon and the ruffle. Pull the gathering slightly, and secure it with stitches.

Diagram 20

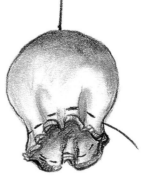

U-Gather and Variations

Single U-Gather Petals and Flat Rosettes

Diagram 21

Depending on the length of the ribbon used, the stitch pattern will look like a U-shape or a very stretched version of a U-shape. If the ribbon is wired, remove the bottom wire. Sew the stitch pattern shown, and gather it to the desired shape. If you are making a petal, gather the ribbon tightly. In some cases, the ribbon you gather will be used as a ruffle and placed around an existing rose center. If you are making a flat rosette, then continue on to Diagrams 22 and 23.

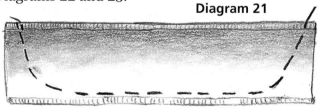

Diagram 21

Diagram 22

When making a flat rosette, gather the ribbon length and overlap the ends by hooking one end over the other. Make sure all of the raw edges are brought into the back of the circle you are creating. The needle and thread will be at the back.

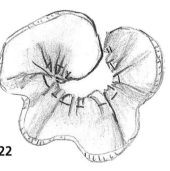

Diagram 22

Diagram 23

Hold the overlapped ribbon between your thumb and first finger, and tighten the gathering by pulling down on the thread. Secure this gathering at the center with a few backstitches. Cover the center with seed beads.

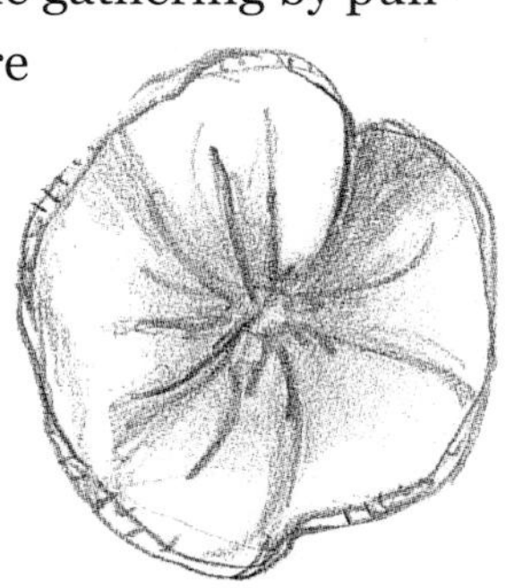

Diagram 23

Diagram 24

This is a tightly gathered basic petal.

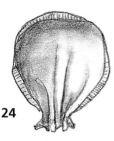

Diagram 24

Diagram 25

This is a tightly gathered miniature leaf. Your leaf may look different based on the ribbon used in the project.

Diagram 25

Diagram 26

This is a small basic rosette.

Diagram 26

Diagram 27

This is a larger silk ribbon rosette.

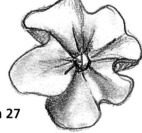

Diagram 27

Diagram 28

This is a multilayered or spiral rosette. The look of the spiral rosette will vary depending on the width, length and style of the ribbon used. Gather the ribbon using the stitch pattern in Diagram 21, then stitch one end of the gathered ribbon to the center of a circle of crinoline. Coil the remaining gathered ribbon in a spiral, and secure these layers of ribbon to the crinoline with stitches. Cover the center with seed beads, a button or another small ribbon flower. Cut away the excess crinoline.

Diagram 28

Variation 1 – Upright Coil Roses

Diagram 29

If the ribbon is wired, remove the bottom wire. Fold down the right end of the ribbon, and then fold the ribbon across on itself.

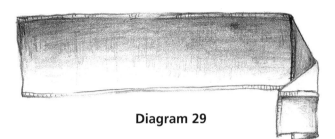

Diagram 29

Diagram 30

Roll the folded end into a tight cylinder — roll until the opening at the top of the cylinder goes to a round shape, and then stop, or you'll waste ribbon. Secure the cylinder with stitches at the base of the cylinder, and sew the stitch pattern shown. Your ribbon type and length may differ from the diagram. In some cases where the ribbon is too short, skip the stitching and just roll the ribbon up into a cylinder, and you'll have made a bud.

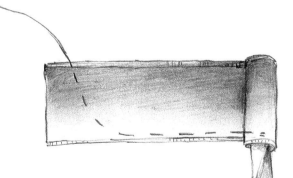

Diagram 30

Diagram 31

Gather the ribbon to about one-third of its original length, but don't secure the gathering just yet. Test the degree of gathering needed for the rose shape you want by coiling the gathered ribbon on itself. Once the rose shape is as you like it, secure the gathering. Sew through all of the layers at the base of the rose so the center of the rose doesn't pop out. Note: If the rose is large, construct it on crinoline. Sew the coiled center to crinoline, and then coil the gathered ribbon around the center. Stitch the coils in place, and tuck the gathered raw edge under a ruffle.

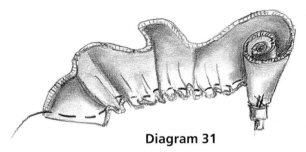

Diagram 31

Diagram 32

This is a finished small upright coil rose. Your finished rose may be small or large, depending on the width and length of ribbon used.

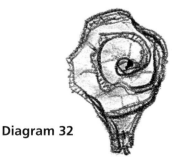

Diagram 32

Variation 2 –
Bottom Two-Thirds Fold Edge

Diagram 33

Use this variation if you want to have the look of two rows of ruffled petals. Fold the ribbon up by two-thirds.

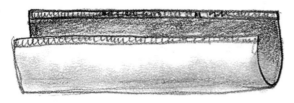

Diagram 33

Diagram 34

Stitch the U-gather pattern.

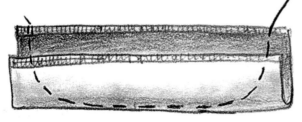

Diagram 34

Diagram 35

Gather the ribbon, and form it into a flat rosette. Secure it in the same manner as for a single flat rosette. Separate and fluff the layers of ribbon.

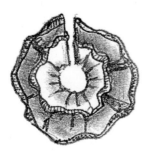

Diagram 35

Variation 3 –
Rolled Edge for Cabochon Rose

Diagram 36

If the ribbon is wired, remove the bottom wire only. Roll the top edge of the ribbon down very tightly to two-thirds of its original width. For example: 1½"-wide ribbon will be rolled down to a 1" width. Pin the ribbon at the edges to keep it from unrolling. Stitch the pattern.

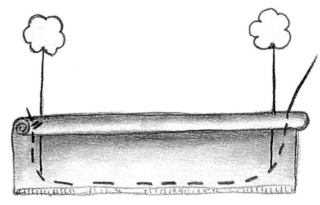

Diagram 36

Diagram 37

Gather the ribbon, and secure it. Sometimes it is easier to secure the gathering after the petal has been placed over the rose center.

Diagram 37

Diagram 38

Place the petal over the middle of the rose center, and bring the cupped shape around the crinoline. Stitch the petal in place. Be sure the raw ends of the petal are positioned under the crinoline. In other words, the rose center and crinoline fit inside the cupped petal. All of the petals are attached in this manner. Note: The rose center is most often an upright coil rose or a folded rose that is stitched to a small circle of crinoline.

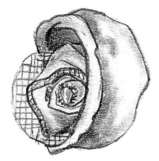

Diagram 38

Diagram 39

When stitching the remaining petals over the rose center, overlap them so only one row of petals is formed.

Diagram 39

Continuous U-Gathers and Four-Petal U-Gather

Diagram 40

If the ribbon is wired, remove the bottom wire. Fold the ribbon into four equal sections, leaving ⅛" margins at each end of the ribbon, and sew the stitch pattern shown. Note how the thread continuously goes over the top of the ribbon edge to connect the U-gather segments. This makes the gathering of the ribbon easier.

Diagram 40

Diagram 41

If you are making blossoms, regardless of the ribbon style or size used, gather the ribbon tightly to form four petals. Form this into a circle, and join the first and last petal together. Note: If you are using stamens for the center, then insert the stamens before joining the petals together. The stamen stems can be left long, as they will be hidden under other flowers and leaves in a composition. If you are using beads for the center, then add the beads after the petals are joined. The blossom will look different according to the ribbon used. If the petals are to be used on a tea rose, do not secure the gathering until the petals have been fitted around the rose center.

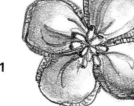

Diagram 41

Folding Ribbon

Basic Flat Bud

Diagram 42

If the ribbon is wired, remove the wire from the bottom edge. Fold the ribbon across itself as shown.

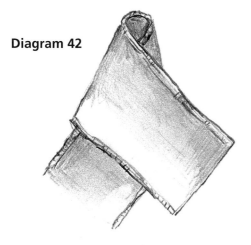

Diagram 42

Diagram 43

Curl the left edge of the ribbon. Pin the roll in place. If you are stemming the bud, insert a piece of wire or gimp between the layers of ribbon so it's caught in the stitching that follows. Note: By skipping the curled edge, a simpler bud or a leaf can be made, then finished, using Diagrams 44 and 45.

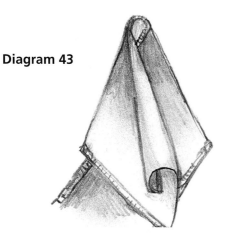

Diagram 43

Diagram 44

Stitch and gather across the layers of ribbon as shown. Be sure to stitch through all three layers of ribbon. Note: It is easier to stitch from the backside of the ribbon where you can follow the line at the base of the triangle. Pull the gathering tightly, wrap the thread once around the stitching, and secure it.

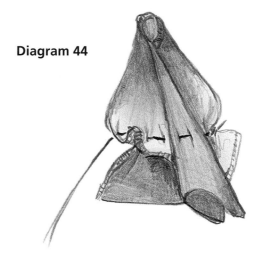

Diagram 44

Diagram 45

The finished bud. If the bud is exposed in a composition, then it will need a calyx; see Stems and Calyxes.

Diagram 45

Vintage Flat Rose

Diagram 46

The rose is made from one length of ribbon and a series of turns to create folds, which are stitched to a circle or square of crinoline. Cut the crinoline according to the project specifications; however, larger is better, as it can always be cut down if the rose is smaller than planned. Make a knot at the end of a length of ribbon, leaving very little tail. Sew the knot to the center of the crinoline circle. Sew a stitch beside the top right corner of the knot. This will act as a pivot when you are turning the ribbon tail to make the first fold. With your finger and thumb, hold the ribbon at this stitch, and turn the ribbon down to near the short knot tail so a fold is created. This is about a one-quarter turn.

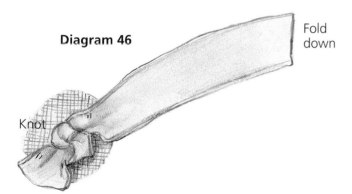

Diagram 46

Fold down

Knot

Diagram 47

Secure the first fold with stitches as shown. Make a second fold as you did the first fold by simply turning the ribbon another one-quarter turn (and creating a fold) toward the bottom left corner of the knot rose center.

Diagram 47

Diagram 48

Secure the second fold with stitches as shown. Turn the ribbon another one-quarter turn, and create another fold.

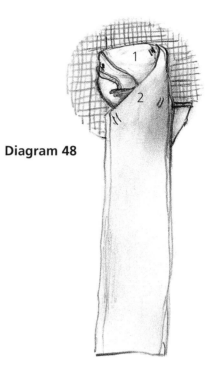

Diagram 48

Diagram 49

Secure the third fold with stitches as shown. Turn the ribbon another one-quarter turn and create a fourth fold.

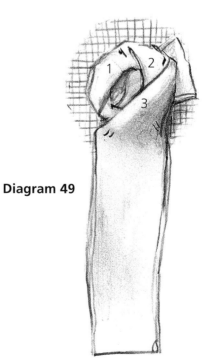

Diagram 49

Diagram 50

Secure the fourth fold with stitches as shown. You have completed one round of folds. Continue to fold the ribbon with one-quarter turns for a few more rounds. As the rose gets bigger, you may need to make one-fifth turns for the folds. When you've completed the rose according to the project specifications, trim away the excess crinoline, if any, and fold the ribbon tail to the underside of the crinoline. In some cases, the outer row of folds will hang over the edge of the crinoline circle. Tack this excess ribbon under the circle when sewing the rose to the project.

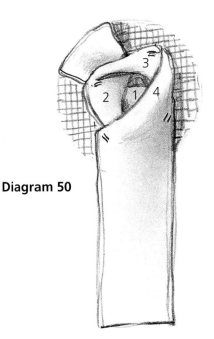

Diagram 50

Diagram 51

This is the finished rose. The rose may look smaller or larger, depending on the project specifications.

Diagram 51

Folded Rose

Diagram 52

Your ribbon may be larger or smaller in width and length than what is shown in the diagrams. Fold down the right end of the ribbon.

Diagram 52

Diagram 53

Fold the ribbon across once on itself.

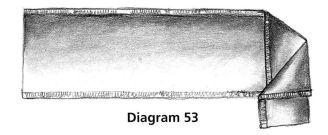

Diagram 53

Diagram 54

Tightly roll the ribbon until the top of the ribbon just forms a round cylinder. Stitch the base to secure the ribbon folds. Do not cut the thread.

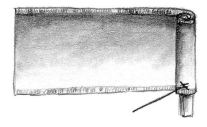

Diagram 54

Diagram 55

Fold the ribbon on the left toward the back so the fold forms a 45-degree angle. Tilt the coiled ribbon cylinder so it rests almost at the end of the diagonal fold. A large cavity should be evident between the fold and the cylinder. The top of the cylinder should not rise higher than the folded edge of the ribbon.

Diagram 55

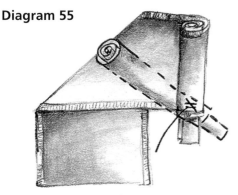

Diagram 56

Roll the ribbon cylinder beyond the diagonal (about a three-quarter turn) until the excess ribbon is situated to the left of the cylinder again. Secure the new folds of the ribbon cylinder. You'll notice that these folds at the base of the rose will creep up higher and higher as the rose grows. Remember to keep the top folds of this rose level in order to avoid a telescoping rose center. Repeat Diagrams 55 and 56 until the size of rose is reached.

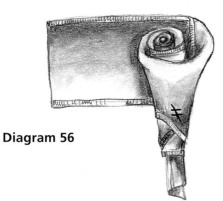

Diagram 56

Diagram 57

Finish the rose by folding down the last few inches of ribbon into the underside of the rose and securing it with stitches. Closely trim the ribbon tail from the base of the rose. Your rose may look larger or smaller than what is shown, depending on the ribbon required for the project.

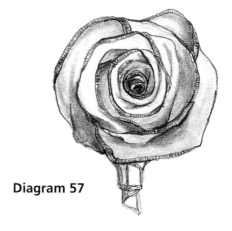

Diagram 57

113

Petals

Rolled Corner Petal

Diagram 58

Fold the ribbon in half.

Diagram 58

Diagram 60

Roll this folded corner once. Secure the roll with a few hidden backstitches from beneath the roll of ribbon. Sometimes, it is easier to open the layers of ribbon and make these stitches from the inside. Be careful not to let the stitches show on the front of the petal — the nonrolled side. Secure the stitches, and cut the thread.

Diagram 60

Diagram 59

Work on the back of the petal first. Make a small fold in one corner. How big you make this fold will determine if the finished petal is round-topped or pointed. Small corners will give a more rounded petal shape.

Diagram 59

Diagram 61

Fold in the other corner.

Diagram 61

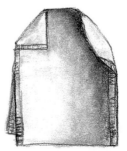

Diagram 62

Roll this fold once again. Secure the roll with a few hidden backstitches from beneath the roll of ribbon. Cut the thread.

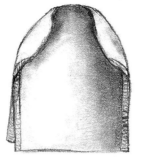

Diagram 62

Diagram 63

Narrow the bottom of the petal with two pleats, or just gather it across. Secure it with stitches. This is the back view of the completed petal.

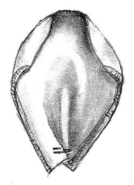

Diagram 63

Diagram 64

This is the front view of a completed petal. The petal will have a cupped shape.

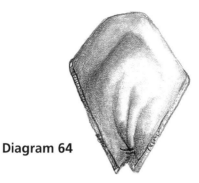

Diagram 64

Diagram 65

To make a rose, stitch the first petal to the rose center (or stem of stamens), keeping the top of the petal above the top of the rose center. The front side of the petal will be facing the stamens or rose center. Overlap and stitch each consecutive petal to the previous petal, continuing in a clockwise manner until all of the petals have been stitched on. The tops of the petals should be positioned slightly higher than the top of the rose center. To secure and tighten the rose, push the needle and thread through all of the layers of ribbon near the base of the rose several times. If the rose is stemmed, cover the raw edges of the petals and the wire stem with bias-cut silk ribbon.

Diagram 65

Side-Roll Petals

Single Side-Roll Petal

Diagram 66

The size of the petal will vary from the diagram according to the width and length of the ribbon used in the project. If the ribbon is wired, remove the bottom wire. Make a very tiny corner fold.

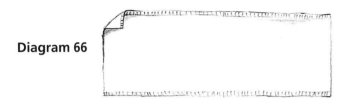

Diagram 66

Diagram 67

Roll this corner tightly until the bottom edge of the roll reaches the bottom edge of the ribbon. If you are having trouble making these tiny rolls, try rolling the ribbon around a toothpick.

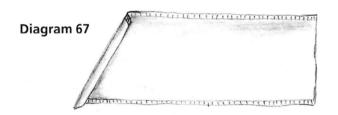

Diagram 67

Diagram 68

Sew three tiny backstitches in the back of the roll to secure it. Be sure the stitches are not visible on the front of the roll.

Diagram 68

Diagram 69

Sew the stitch pattern shown, then gather tightly.

Diagram 69

Diagram 70

This is the finished petal. These petals make a button rose.

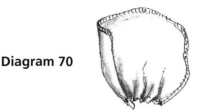

Diagram 70

Diagram 71

To assemble a button rose using these petals, overlap and sew three petals in an arc shape to a piece of crinoline. Be sure the rolls are facing you. Sew the stamens over the petals.

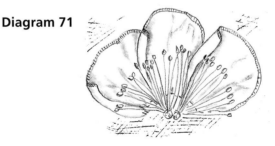

Diagram 71

Diagram 72

Cover the stamens with a large button. Sew a fourth and fifth petal to each side of the button, making sure the raw edges are tucked under the button. Cup these petals over the button. Sew the sixth petal — a double side-roll petal, made the same way as Diagram 77 — between the front petals. Trim the excess crinoline.

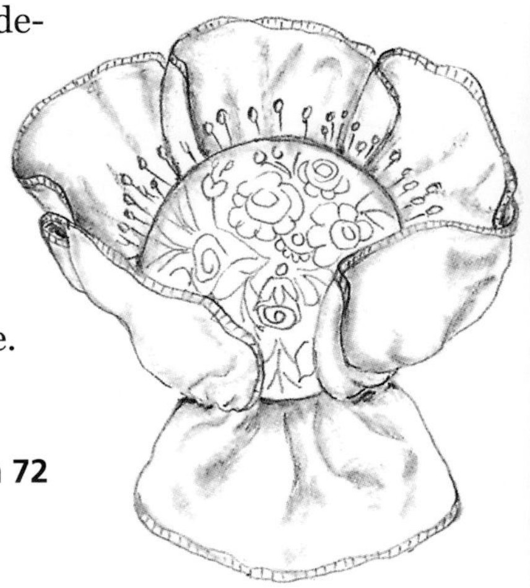

Diagram 72

Double Side-Roll Petal

Diagram 73

The size of the petal may vary from the diagram according to the width and length of the ribbon used in the project. If the ribbon is wired, remove the bottom wire. Make a very tiny corner fold.

Diagram 73

Diagram 74

Roll this corner tightly until the bottom edge of the roll reaches the bottom edge of the ribbon. If you are having trouble making these tiny rolls, try rolling the ribbon around a toothpick.

Diagram 74

Diagram 75

Sew three tiny backstitches in the back of the roll to secure it. Be sure the stitches are not visible on the front of the roll.

Diagram 75

Diagram 76

Fold and roll the opposite side of the ribbon. Secure the roll with stitches the same as the first roll. Stitch across the bottom of the ribbon.

Diagram 76

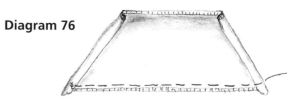

Diagram 77

Tightly gather the stitching so a petal shape is formed. The rolls are shown on the front of the petal. Twelve of these petals make a vintage petal rose when sewn to crinoline.

Diagram 77

Diagram 78

This is a finished vintage petal rose. To assemble this rose, sew eight petals in a circle to crinoline. Thinking of a clock face, sew two petals at the 11 o'clock and 1 o'clock positions over the back petals. Sew a small folded rose center over these two petals. Sew two petals over the folded rose; make sure that the raw edges are hidden underneath. An optional 13th petal may be added over the front two petals.

Diagram 78

Leaves

Prairie Point Leaf

Diagram 79

If you are using ombre ribbon, decide which color edge you want as the point of the leaf. If the ribbon is wired, remove the bottom wire. Mark the halfway point of the ribbon length, and fold down one end of the ribbon at that point.

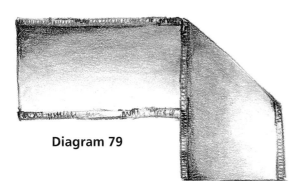

Diagram 79

Diagram 80

Fold the other half of the ribbon down.

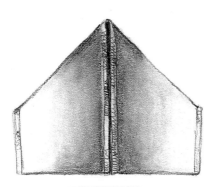

Diagram 80

Diagram 81

Gather across the bottom, going through all of the layers of ribbon. If you turn the ribbon to the back, use the bottom of the triangle (bottom edge of the ribbon) as a guide to stitch on. If you are stemming the leaf, slip a 32-gauge wire between the ribbon layers at the stitch line before tightening the gathering.

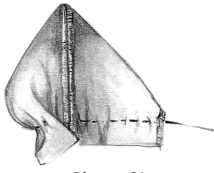

Diagram 81

Diagram 82

Gather the stitching very tightly, wrap your thread around the base of the leaf once, pull it tightly, and secure the wrap with a few stitches. Cut the thread. Trim the excess ribbon from the base of the leaf. If the leaf was stemmed, cover it with bias-cut silk ribbon or floral tape.

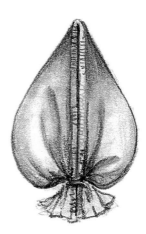

Diagram 82

Crossover Leaf

Diagram 83

If the ribbon is wired, remove the bottom wire. Fold the ribbon across on itself.

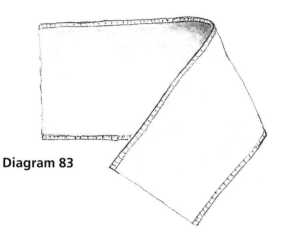

Diagram 83

Diagram 84

Fold over the other side of the ribbon. Stitch and gather across the layers of ribbon as shown. Be sure to stitch through all three layers of ribbon. Note: It is easier to stitch from the back side of the ribbon where you can follow the line at the base of the triangle. If you are stemming this leaf, insert a 3" piece of 32-gauge wire into the stitch line so it is caught in the gathering. Cover the stem with bias-cut silk ribbon.

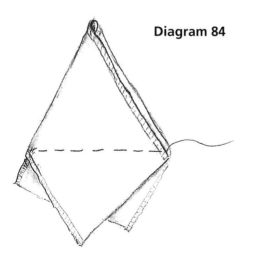

Diagram 84

Diagram 85

This is the finished leaf. This leaf technique also can be used as a flower bud when a ribbon color other than green is used.

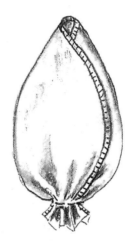

Diagram 85

Half-Round Leaf

Diagram 86

This leaf can be made with narrow or wide ribbons. If the ribbon is wired, remove the bottom wire. Sew the U-gather stitch pattern shown, and pull the gathering tightly. Secure the gathering. Trim the excess ribbon from each end.

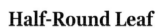

Diagram 86

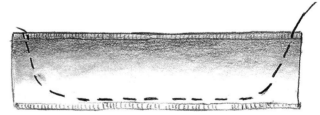

Your leaf will look like one of these samples depending on the ribbon used.

Curve Leaf

Diagram 87

Your ribbon may be much smaller than what is shown in the diagrams. If you are using an ombre ribbon, decide which color the edge is to be. The color edge you choose will be opposite the stitch pattern. If the ribbon has a ruffled edge, this also will be opposite the stitch pattern. If the ribbon is wired, remove the wire along the side that will be stitched. Fold the ribbon in half. Stitch the curved pattern shown starting at the fold end of the ribbon; the fold is the point of the finished leaf.

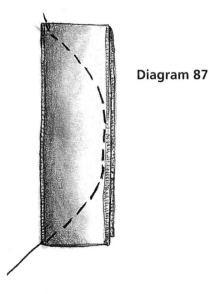

Diagram 87

Diagram 88

Pull the stitching thread just until the gathering appears to be in a straight line. The top of the ribbon will now be curved. Do not secure the gathering yet.

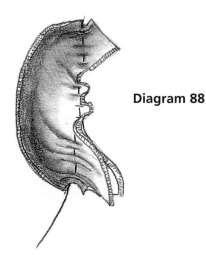

Diagram 88

Diagram 89

Open the leaf. Adjust the gathering to the shape and fullness of leaf desired. Secure the gathering.

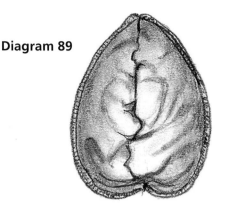

Diagram 89

Diagram 90

Flatten the tab at the point of the leaf on the back, and secure it with a stitch. Skip this if the ribbon leaf you are making is very small. Trim the excess ribbon from the bottom of the leaf. Style the leaf by pushing the gathering away from the point and toward the bottom of the leaf. If the leaf is to be stemmed, follow the instructions for the boat leaf, Diagram 95.

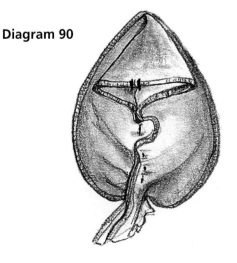

Diagram 90

Boat Leaf

Diagram 91

If you are using an ombre ribbon, decide which color the edge is to be. The color edge you choose will be opposite the stitch pattern. If the ribbon has a ruffled edge, this also will be opposite the stitch pattern. If the ribbon is wired, remove the wire along the side that will be stitched. Fold the ribbon in half.

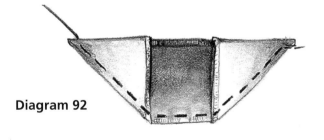

Diagram 91

Diagram 92

Turn up the bottom corners of the ribbon so a boat shape is formed. The fold end is the tip of the leaf. Begin the stitching pattern from the folded point on the right and continue along the bottom edge of the ribbon to the other point.

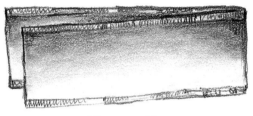

Diagram 92

Diagram 93

Pull the gathering thread so the bottom of the boat goes straight. Don't secure the gathering just yet.

Diagram 93

Diagram 94

Open the ribbon, and test the gathering until the leaf is the shape you want. Secure the gathering with stitches. Trim off the two triangular ribbon tabs at the back of the leaf. Style the leaf by pushing the gathering away from the point and toward the bottom of the leaf.

Diagram 94

Diagram 95

If you are stemming a leaf, lay the wire on the back of the leaf, and whipstitch it to the spine of the leaf. Cover the stem wire with bias-cut silk ribbon or floral tape.

Diagram 95

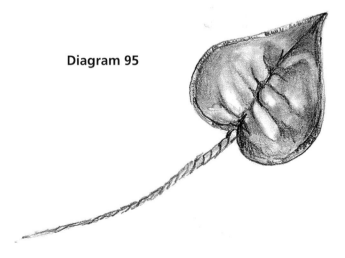

Bibliography

This brightly colored tea rose brooch is made with textured wire-edge ribbon.

"Ribbon and Fabric Trimmings," Woman's Institute of Domestic Arts and Sciences Inc., 1925.

"Ribbon Art," Volume 1, No. 1, Ribbon Art Publishing Company of America Inc., 1923.

"Ribbon Art," Volume 1, No. 2, Ribbon Art Publishing Company of America Inc.

"Ribbon Art," Volume 1, No. 3, Ribbon Art Publishing Company of America Inc.

"Old Fashioned Ribbon Trimmings and Flowers," Mary Brooks Picken, Dover Publications, 1993, originally published in 1922.

"In Style," Jean L. Druessedow, Metropolitan Museum of Art.

"The Opulent Era," Elizabeth Ann Coleman, Thames and Hudson and The Brooklyn Museum, 1990.

"Best Dressed," Dilys E. Blum and Kristina H. Haughland, Philadelphia Museum of Art, 1997.

"The Half-doll," Volumes 1, 2, 3 and 4, Shona and Marc Lorrin, Walsworth Publishing Company, 1999, 2001, 2003, 2005.

"The Collector's Encyclopedia of Half-dolls," Frieda Marion and Norma Werner, Crown Publishers Inc., 1979.

"The Century of Hats," Susie Hopkins, Chartwell Books, 1999.

"Millinery For Every Woman," Georgina Kerr Kay, Lacis Publications, Berkeley Calif., 1992, originally published 1926.

Resources

Retail

Autographed ribbonwork books, DVD, kits and ribbons are available from Helen Gibb Design.

A half-doll pincushion showcases ribbon flowers on an antique lace apron.

Helen Gibb Design Inc.
1002 Turnberry Circle
Louisville, CO 80027
Web: www.helengibb.com
E-mail: helen@helengibb.com
Phone: 303-673-0949
Fax: 303-926-0065

All of the ribbonwork supplies and ribbons used in this book are available through Helen Gibb Design. Purchase ribbon starter kits, needles, thread, crinoline, ribbons, trims, embellishing packs, porcelain half-dolls, kits, fabric prints, laces and more online or by mail order or phone. Signed copies of Helen's books and Helen's ribbonwork DVD are also available.

Helen teaches ribbon workshops internationally, and within the United States. She also organizes and teaches at her two ribbon retreats in Colorado — one in the spring and one in the fall. Please visit her Web site www.helengibb.com, for more information, and to buy ribbonwork supplies online.

Send $7 if requesting a product brochure and $7 if requesting a ribbon brochure, plus two first-class stamps, to Helen Gibb Design Inc. at the address above.

Wholesale

Quilters' Resource Inc.
3702 Prairie Lake Court
Aurora, IL 60504
Web site: www.quiltersresource.com
Phone: 630-820-5695
Fax: 630-851-2136
Crinoline, pins, needles, thread, stamens and
French ribbons

Renaissance Ribbons
P.O. Box 699
Oregon House, CA 95962
Web site: www.renaissanceribbons.com
Phone: 530-692-0842
Fax: 530-692-0915
Importer of high-quality French ribbons

Mokuba
55 W. 39th St.
New York, NY 10018
Phone: 212-869-8900
Fax: 212-869-8970
Importer of beautiful Japanese ribbons and
flower trims

Artemis
5155 Myrtle Ave.
Eureka, CA 95503
Web site: www.artemisinc.com
Phone: 888-233-5187
Fax: 707-442-8453
E-mail: artemissilk@aol.com
The largest and best source for Hanah Silk
bias-cut silk ribbons

Other Resources

Visionary Reflections
Brandon Wade
1855 S. Pearl St, No. 1
Denver, CO 80210
Web site: www.visionaryreflections.com
Phone: 303-519-3070
Specializing in how-to videography, video biography,
photography and Web site design

The Fuzzy Antler
901 Front St., Suite 100
Louisville, CO 80027
Web site: www.thefuzzyantler.com
Phone: 303-666-7864
Fax: 303-666-7865
An exquisite shop filled with European antiques and
home furnishings

Krause Publications
700 E. State St.
Iola, WI 54990
Web site: www.krause.com
Phone: 888-457-2873
Fax: 715-445-4087
Publisher of quality how-to books for sewing, quilting
and other crafts, as well as other hobby interests

*Ribbon roses are made with a variety
of ribbon styles and techniques.*

Index

Chatelaines were commonly used for keeping treasured sewing tools in one place. This chatelaine, with a needle book and a strawberry pincushion, is made from silk ribbons woven through ivory rings. Circa 1920.

A bas relief half-doll head is the centerpiece for this factory-made pincushion. Circa 1920.

About the Author

Helen Gibb was born in Sydney, Australia, and now lives in the United States.

"Growing up in Australia during the 1950s and 1960s, I wasn't particularly interested in sewing or embroidery," says Helen. "The only sewing project I finished in primary school was a shower cap and an apron!"

Helen's ribbonwork journey started in the late 1990s with the purchase of an Edwardian driving hat, and later, a black mourning bonnet complete with black ribbon embellishments. An antique book on old millinery techniques was also purchased, and in the back of that book were some simplified instructions on how to make a ribbon rose. Since then, Helen has acquired many old books about ribbonwork and some lovely samples of vintage ribbon flowers and items from the 1920s, many of which are shown on the pages of this book.

With a vast store of self-taught ribbon techniques and access to ribbons from France and Japan, Helen's incredible talents in ribbonwork are evident throughout the pages of this book, and her other three ribbon books: "The Secrets of Fashioning Ribbon Flowers," "Heirloom Ribbonwork," and "Ribbonwork The Complete Guide." Helen also has created the DVD "Beginner's Guide to Ribbonwork."

Helen's ribbonwork has been showcased in numerous magazines in the United States and Australia, including Better Homes and Gardens magazine, Doll Costuming magazine and Embroidery and Cross Stitch magazine. On television, Helen has been a regular guest on HGTV's "The Carol Duvall Show." She also has appeared on PBS' "Creative Living," and on TV news programs in Denver.

Helen lives in Colorado with her husband, Jim, where they enjoy the Rocky Mountains. When she's not doing ribbonwork, Helen loves to read. She also sings with the Rocky Mountain Chorale.

Visit Helen's Web site, www.helengibb.com, for books, her DVD, ribbonwork supplies and more information about ribbonwork retreats and classes.

Have fun with ribbonwork! Not only is the bride's gown decorated with ribbonwork roses and streamers, so are the hood and trunk of the bridal car.

Countless Project Ideas
You Can Create With Ribbon

Ribbonwork:
The Complete Guide
Techniques for Making
Ribbon Flowers and Trimmings
by Helen Gibb

Ribbonwork comes to life in this appealing guide, featuring 20 beautiful projects to craft for heirlooms or gifts. Materials overviews, a "Ribbon Length Guide," easy-to-follow directions and an inspirational gallery are included!

HC w/concealed spiral • 5⅝ x 7⅝
256 pages • 150 color photos,
plus illus.
Item# RWPR • $29.99

New Ideas in Ribbon Craft
Susan Niner Janes

Learn to use ribbon to create gorgeous home décor projects quickly and inexpensively. Chapters on ribbon flowers, embroidery, weaving and bows make way for 22 exciting projects, including pillows, baby blankets, purses and more.

Softcover • 8½ x 11 • 128 pages
20 b&w illus. • 250 color illus.
Item# 32323 • $22.99

Heirloom Ribbonwork
Ribbon Creations
for the Next Generation
by Helen Gibb

This illustrated step-by-step technique guide teaches the basics of ribbon flower construction and features 27 projects.

Softcover • 8¼ x 10⅞ • 128 pages
150 illus. • 100 color photos
Item# HLRIB • $24.95

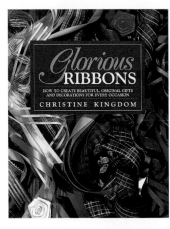

Glorious Ribbons
by Christine Kingdom

Weave it. Pleat it. Fold it. Then try embroidery and appliqué—all with ribbon. Bows, baskets, roses, garlands, and 50 other projects provide hours of crafting pleasure and fill the home with affordable accents and exquisitely personal touches.

Softcover • 8¼ x 10⅞ • 128 pages
color throughout
Item# GLRI • $19.95

The Secrets of Fashioning
Ribbon Flowers
Heirlooms For the Next Generation
by Helen Gibb

Learn the techniques needed to make 15 flowers, and then how to incorporate the stunning blossoms into jewelry, home décor, wearables, handbags, and more.

Softcover • 8¼ x 10⅞ • 128 pages
150 b&w illus. • 100 color photos
Item# FFFGD • $24.95

Simply Beautiful
Ribboncraft
Heidi Boyd

Even complete beginners can find success crating the pretty home accents, gifts, cards, baby items and holiday projects found in this book. 50 step-by-step projects and 15 variations for every taste and skill level.

Softcover • 8½ x 11 • 128 pages
20 b&w illus. • 250 color illus.
Item# 33107 • $19.99